Ghetto Blessings

By Carlos Robinson

ODF Publishing House

ISBN: 978-0-578-00080-0

Table of Contents

Ma Johnson 5
Prism Light 9
A talk to ease the pain 11
Life out of Darkness 21
Optimal Resolution 23
Freedom 2 25
Freedom 1 27
A King has Died (When kings die) 29
No Name 31
Ghetto Blessings: Understanding 41
The Old Man and Me 45
The Prodigal Son 51
If I don't wake up..... 53
Facing the Truth 57
A Tear for Tiffany 61
Seeking Forgiveness 63
I Am so Blessed 65
My "Ma" 67
Anger 71
A Prayer 73
Molestation 75
Where God Abides 79
Prison 81
Cracked Lives 83
A Lump of Coal 87
Ghetto Blessings: Redemption 89
Miracle Lessons: The Blessings Unfold 93
About The Author 97
Excerpt From Open Heart Surgery 99

Ma Johnson

"Son, no matter what you get in this life it don't mean much if you didn't work for it."

Ma Johnson was a time worn old woman. Nobody really knew how old because her demeanor was such that you feared asking her personally, so the neighborhood rumors abounded that she was 107. Maybe sometimes through the grunts and moans you could see it, but for the most part the way she carried herself suggested she was winning a very slow race against age. See, even though age and wrinkles had kidnapped the beauty she once flaunted as a youth if you looked closely at her frame or listened for the moments when she would find that sultry womanly deep voice that was hidden beneath parched years, you would actually see as well as feel her stately beauty, charm and grace. She was a portly woman. Age and retirement attacked her once frail figure with far too many pounds for her to evade. The extra weight looked so out of place. She had silky black hair soft as cotton, overtaken by gray strands that were twisted into plaits on either side of her perfectly oval face. Today as I write this each minute detail of that day has resurfaced; the formation of cumulus clouds that marched barely noticeable across the sky; the smells of the neighborhood, a mix of home cooking, exhaust fumes and mowed grass. These are the sounds of life that surrounded us that day, but most importantly the very words she spoke resonate in my mind as though she were saying them right now. It is like she had waited her entire life to say them to me that day.

We sat on her porch, me at her feet sipping the icy freshness of her home brewed lemonade while she rocked effortlessly in an old wooden rocking chair. I sipped the drink with huge gulps of air, batting my eyes fiercely as 9 year olds do sometimes. In between blinks I stole glances at this woman the whole neighborhood affectionately knew as "Ma Johnson".

"I 'member yo' gran'daddy Johnson would sit there just like you doin' right now and stare off into this ole world lookin' for som'thin. I don't rightly know to this day what it was or if he ever found it. Son I don't know why the Lord done choose you? But... oh sweet Jesus! He done told me you gotta' go through some thangs in your journey. You gonna go through the fire hear me?! You gonna' see thangs and do thangs that av'age people like myself will never understand or maybe even believe! But you just gotta' keep goin'. You gotta keep yo' head up and keep goin' cause if you stop.... that ole devil gonna try an convince you that life just ain't woth livin' no more."

This all sounded kind of inappropriate to me at the time, prior to me sitting down. August heat was bearing down on me as I pushed an old Briggs and Stratton mower, furiously cutting her foot tall grass for free. Maybe it was the fact my paper route didn't yield the profits I expected and out of all the yards I'd cut that day, buying that wonderfully purple Sears and Roebuck bicycle still seemed further away than I cared to see.

She reached for me with a trembling cracked walnut brown skinned hand, shuffling laboriously in the chair to get closer to me. I didn't think twice about taking her hand in my own in an attempt to be the gentleman by helping her to rise. But that wasn't her purpose as she pulled me to her bosom and wrapped her arms around me. As my head lay there pressed tightly to her breast I could hear her heart beating slow rhythmic fluxes of love. She took me by the shoulders and held me up mere inches from her face then kissed my forehead tenderly and whispered,

"But if you keep goin', oooo Lord Jesus! THANK YOU! If you keep followin' the Lord son, one day all your stories will be mem'ries that gonna' set yo' soul free! God loves you son, no matter what you do."

She then fell back into the comfort of the chair and once again on cue the effortless rocking back and forth commenced. I gulped down the last of my lemonade and headed back to finish mowing the foot high grass. "God loves you too Ma Johnson." I spoke into the humid windless air, and then fired the prattled roar of the Briggs and Stratton to life.

That was 36 years ago but in my heart and mind it seems like only yesterday. "Thank you Ma Johnson."

Prism Light

"I sat on this one particular night looking for God amongst the things of the world, the buildings, trees, the many stars in the expanse of sky. I sat there crowded by my sins, feeling as if they were looking back at me too, calling me a "fool", asking me," How do you expect to see something that can not be seen!?" So I fought my mind for freedom because I couldn't stand how close sin was to me. Each breath I took, feeling as if it would be my last, was held at length, my chest tight and constricted as if the mighty pressure of a python were squeezing my ribs and suffocating the life from me. My head aching, throbbing, with the constant heavy bass beat of ghetto confusion that caused my eyes to water but allowed no tears came out. I screamed from deep in my soul,

"LEAVE ME ALONE!!!, WHY DO YOU TORMENT ME SO?!". The only answer that came was the wailing whine of a siren approaching and this angered me even more.

"GOD?!, SHOW ME YOUR FACE! I HAVE TO SEE YOUR FACE!, WHY DO YOU HIDE FROM ME?!" This is what I cried out in the hollows of my mind.

A gunshot was fired off breaking the eerie silence of the world around me mingling with the clouded noise of the streets and echoing through the expanse of tall buildings that are worn and dilapidated by time.

"I HATE THIS PLACE!!!" I cried out with pain, my anger now so fused I couldn't focus on anything but filth and poverty.

I sat on this particular night, "Ghetto King" on my throne steps of concrete, dried blood and spittle. As cold swirled about me, biting at my exposed flesh like hungry piranha, I wondered...."how can I see God when I don't even know if He truly exists?"

I sat there, holding up the 400 pound weight of corruption that bore down on me with a force just short of crushing me. "I want to kill you..." it said softly.

"YOU CANT!", I shouted aloud. "I CANT DIE MAN! I WON'T DIE, BECAUSE if I do then you'll have lost a king, then who'll lead these people? WHO'LL BEFRIEND MY SINS?!" Then I bowed my head shaking bodily from the pain, frustration and anger. I cursed the world for electing me "notorious". Two winos staggered by cozy in their dirty rags of clothing, and holding bottles wrapped in wrinkled brown paper bags. I cursed who I was and felt I had to get away before I hurt someone else...before I went mad! "We won't let you go! We're yours forever fool!" All the voices of sin and perdition exclaimed in unison, and with such thunderous harmony that I jumped and chills shot through my being. On that night I saw my eventual imprisonment and death as fear sat beside me smoking a blunt, smiling at me, trying to be my friend to keep me from knowing it was I that frightened it. I never saw salvation. I never saw God either, physically. But now, today I know that He was there just as he is now and has always been; spiritually. Yet.....I'm still looking."

A talk to ease the pain

I was tired that evening but I still ran toward home with a stride that mimicked a thoroughbred in the last quarter mile of the Preakness. There was only a few minutes left before darkness and the streetlights would light up the night of the neighborhood. Needless to say that was my curfew. I don't care where I was, basketball or band practices had to end with enough time for me to get home before the streetlights came on. Either get home or get punished and at this time in my life punishment wasn't an option. Since I left for school so early in the morning, I always had to leave just a couple of minutes to stop at the playground just to see who was out and what had transpired in the "hood" while I was away. For two reasons my mother would transport me to the upper west side of Richmond to attend pre-high at West Hampton. One reason was because, by now, I had been permanently expelled from Richmond Public Schools and the other reason was because she honestly believed being in this predominantly Caucasian atmosphere would turn me around from the bad behavior which I had been exhibiting. So we often began our days around 4:30 am and she would return home at 5:00 pm, with me not far behind by way of a city bus ride from the west at 5:30. The bus stop was two blocks from the two story Tudor style row house we lived in. If on schedule, it allowed me, just enough time to swing through Norrell Park where all the "who's who" of the neighborhood hung out playing anything from pick up basketball games to checkers and chess. From sun up till' sundown and late into the night Norrell Park always had something going on. Plus, by this time my life had begun to undergo a drastic change. Yeah I was still a prominent basketball player with dreams of going to college and then pro, but I had also began to find another kind of prominence as a "Hustla'" selling quarter ounces of weed I'd bought with money earned while working with my grandfather in construction on the weekends. However, my life began to change far before this evening. I had spent the previous summer of that year with an uncle in New York who was a prominent figure in a heroin operation and a family of dealers, pimps and prostitutes that gave me another sense of what I wanted out of my life. My summer stays with him actually began when I was 10 but he had always kept me uninvolved with his activities until that summer. I was 15.

As I entered the park, the usual people clambered about as a fierce game of basketball echoed shouts of hoarse players and screeches of rubber soled tennis shoes through the air. My "regulars" ran to me like I was a soldier returning home from war. Like they truly missed "me" not the green, weedy substance I carried and sold in plastic sandwich bags. I had to move fast and do my business because this evening the bus ran minutes off schedule which left me little time to socialize. I had to conduct business and move on.

Mr. Lees called out, "HEY SUPA'STAR?!, YOU READY FOR FRIDAY?!", in his usual raspy old voice.

I didn't have time or concentration to respond, because right now my concern was to watch each person approaching me. Even though I was a celebrity, of sorts, in the neighborhood I never forgot that what I sold meant more to some than my status. I was expendable and that was all there is to it. After the last bag was sold I quickly turned and headed toward home. 10 minutes, give or take a few, and the imposed curfew would be broken. "I have time," I thought, as I ambled down the oak tree lined street counting the money I had just made then stuffing it into a pocket of the backpack I wore strapped around one shoulder. Then as I passed an abandoned house just off to my right I heard a familiar voice call out my name.

"LOS!?"

It startled me to the point that my heart raced and instantly I began to perspire. I kept walking, not only because I didn't want to be late, but also because knowing most of the people that hung out in these houses gave me enough reason to believe there to be some truth to the rumors of how desperate these "junkies" were. The voice continued to speak.

"Oh I get it. You all big time basketball star now you don't know your people no more. It's your boy Face, nigga'. Shit! You actin' like you never seen me before!" Face had a distinctive sounding voice. Even though he was barely 35 years of age it sounded much older, strained like someone was choking the life from it. Maybe it was the hardness of his life? Maybe it's just how God intended it to be. But surely if you listened closely one could hear that it had been very stately and profound at some point in his life. But now, it was just a tool he used to get sympathy

I slowed my pace enough for him to approach me but I kept a safe distance. He came closer and as he did I put my right hand into the pocket of the jeans I wore and grasped the .25 caliber semi automatic pistol hidden there. I had never shot at anyone but had fired a few rounds into cans or the air. I had long ago made up my mind that, if need be, I would not hesitate to shoot a live human being. My uncle had warned me that as long as I dealt in the drug business I would always have a target on my back and my pistol was the only friend I had or could trust.

"Shit nigga' you just gonna keep walking or you gonna stop and holla' at yo' boy for a sec' ?!".

There was a plea in his voice I had not heard before, almost like he was asking me to just hear him out this one time. Hear what he had to say.

"Face, man you know I got to get home bro', besides, I don't have nothin left tonight. I'll have to get with you tomorrow.". I said harshly trying to assert my impending manhood through cracked teenage vocal chords.

"Shit nigga' that's what it's all about for you man?! Somebody got to be askin' you for somethin'? Face ain't askin' for nothin' man. I just wanted to converse with you for a sec'.".

The plea became a merciful cry. In my mind all I could see was every time I stopped long enough to talk to him it always ended with me giving him money or drugs, but tonight in my heart I felt he wanted something more substantial. I stopped. As he came close enough for me to smell him in the dimness of street lights I could see the clothes he wore, the dingy white t-shirt and hole ridden jeans, down to grimy white tennis shoes and that full length dirt brown trench coat he wears no matter what. It could be a thousand degrees outside or freezing cold and he wore that coat. Wore it like a badge of honor taking the verbal abuse of those that saw him as a ridiculous clown hooked on crack. That coat was like the glue that held him together, dirt and all.

"Man, sit for a sec, Talk to old Face."

He implored softly. I took a seat between two parked cars trying to be out of plain sight just in case my mother was looking out for me. I knew I was late now but it didn't seem to matter that much because being right here with Face was the important thing. He came and sat beside me. Then took a cigarette butt from a pocket and lit it with a burst of flame from a lighter. In the instant of the flame I got a glimpse at his eyes. They were big and glassy and didn't focus on the flame instead they were peering blankly at my own.

"Face man, I really got to be getting home bro'.". I said sympathetically.

"I know. I know nigga'! Shit, mom will be ok. I'll swing by tomorrow and tell her you was with old Face and she'll be alright. Ok?".

He said that like it would really make a difference him talking to my mother. Maybe he knew something I didn't? See, Face used to be the rising star in our neighborhood everyone knew him as a respectful young man. In the late 60's, and 70's he was the best "b-baller" the state of VA. knew. Every college wanted him and he was pro material with the likes of Julius "Dr. J" Irving, George "The Iceman" Gervin, and Darryl "Chocolate Thunder" Dawkins. His real name is Robert Faison Randall. He was around 6'-1", his hair was curly brown and he maintained a skinny athletic build. What made him great to me was that he was known on every playground in the city. There were those from the old school that told stories of his playground exploits when basketball was king in his life. Now they tell of his exploits to acquire the new king of his soul, crack cocaine. Back when basketball mattered to him he got the nickname "Face" because he would just " take" people no matter height, weight, or skill level, he would just shame people on the court with his moves. My favorite story was how he shook an opponent so bad the guy came clean out of the tennis he wore and tore holes in his socks from one of Faces spinning slam dunks! There was no question how good he was. Just walk through the doors of Maggie Walker High School and down their hall of fame that stretched from the main entrance down the length of the hall to the gymnasium. There were the trophies that etched his greatness on plaques from most valuable player to state championships. His name was on every trophy there. His pictures, from various newspapers and magazines, spattered on the walls along with the many articles about this man, affectionately known as "Face", covered every free space. Then one year his dream came to an end. No one ever talks about what happened, I think because no one really knows. It just did and he became an addict and has been ever since.

"Los, old Face hurtin' tonight.". He said breaking me from my trance of thought.

"I know you all big time now.... shit old Face was big time too nigga'. Bet I can take all you got right now and not even break a sweat on the court nigga'! Yeah, y'all think cause old Face doin' his thing he can't still get busy on the court! But once you got the gift man.... it don't ever go away.".

His voice trailed into the air and he took a long steady drag from the butt then threw it to the ground. As it smoked there we both watched as the mist of white vapor lifted into the air and disappeared into the night. Then our eyes met once again but this time his were more focused and less bulging. Now it felt like he waited for me to tell him something. Like he was trying to will words of encouragement from my being. We both sat there motionless.

"Man....this shit a trip Los.", he said then his head dropped low between his knees. He puffed a deep sigh of regret and misery. "I mean, look at me man! Look at old FACE! FACE NIGGA' !!! The baddest ballA' in ALL the cont'nental united states of theses fuckin' Americas! What the hell happened? I mean, I had it all man, Colleges, pro scouts. You name it, they were knocking my door down to get at me! Then I slipped man.".

I just sat and peered concerned at him and this must have angered him because he snapped," WHAT ARE YOU STARIN' AT MAN!!? What you see somethin' I don't?! Oh, I get it you feel sorry for old Face? You tryin' to see what the hell happened to turn me into this shell of a man?! Life happened my nigga'! Life. I woke up one morning and life was knockin' at my door tellin' me to come along for this ride. I didn't choose this shit man! It chose me."

Suddenly he began to cry. Not tearful sobs but little whimpers of masculinity seeping from his soul. He reached into another pocket and I thought it was to get another butt, instead he removed a slender glass tube. It was charred on each end and had a wad of something black and wiry crammed in one end. He turned it between his fingers like a gum ball. But there was something precious about the way he held it. Like it was delicate and would break if he exerted too much pressure. He turned it and stared at it.

"This is my life now Los. But where did this shit come from? Think about it. What store used to sell these little glass tubes with flowers in them before crack hit the streets!? Now they on every corner! Who thought to put brillo in a piece of glass and smoke it before crack hit OUR streets man?! ".

He then carefully rummaged through another pocket and pulled out a matchbox. He shook it and whatever was inside rattled sounding like a pebble in a small paper cup of cardboard. When he removed the substance I saw it was a piece of crack, tiny almost effervescent in color, so wee that I thought him crazy to even be carrying it.

"This is my life now Los. CRACK!!! From the time I open my eyes " IF" I go to sleep, till' the day I fall the fuck out from exhaustion! I run these streets looking for it. I steal from my momma' to get it. I rob, cheat, lie it don't matter what! All I want is more of this shit man. A fuckin' piece of chemical rules my life man!"

He placed the piece of crack on an end of the glass tube, held it up to his mouth with that end high in the air careful not to drop the small white chunk from it. He sideways glanced at me as I looked intently at his every move. I had never seen anyone use crack before and it seemed so intriguing while in the pit of my stomach I felt disrespected and appalled by his blatant action. He then struck at the lighters cog until in a flamboyant burst of flame produced yellowish/ blue hue. He held it to the crack piece momentarily until it melted then he placed the glass tube into his lips and inhaled softly. I watched as his legs and hands began to tremble involuntarily. His eyes were now glowing orbs, so wide I thought they would pop from his head. The tube filled with smoke as the flame guided by his now shaking hands danced in and out of the opening. The chemical sizzled and crackled like Rice Krispies in a bowl of milk. Then the flame went out and it was silent night all around. Face sat motionless for a moment that to me seemed only to last a couple of seconds but I imagined in his mind time stood still. Then he looked at the now empty glass tube and shook his head with disbelief.

"That's it man." he said low and dejectedly. I just sat staring at him expecting something spectacular from him. It was nothing like the crazed people I had seen on TV cop shows. He didn't rise running down the street or start yelling at the top of his voice anything violent or unintelligible. He just sat there shaking his head. Then he looked me straight in the eyes and said,

"Carlos..... Please promise yourself right now you will never put this glass dick in your mouth man. See, crack don't know nobody. It don't take no prisoners man. It destroys doctors, lawyers, and politicians, white or black this shit don't discriminate. And once it got you in it's grip it don't just let you go. I get so tired of fightin' man. I get so tired of chasin'. Man, I am so tired of all this shit."

In his eyes is the gaze of too many "hits" whether it was from the glass tube or from those that beat him physically for being an addict with no rationale. I could see his suffering. I could feel it in my being, his brown skin about his face drawn tight to reveal the structure of his skull, the flesh beneath his eyes, swollen from lack of rest, his hair nappy and dirty with speckles of grass entangled in matted tresses. In my mind the nightmarish world of addiction warred against his sanity and the latter was losing.

"This shit ain't supposed to be like this goddammit!!", in anger he cursed God but only because he could not understand; he had to blame something besides himself.

"I can't remember how this happened to me." As quick as it arose the anger subsided turning to humility, then pain. From the tears he now cried poured the answer.

I stood and dusted of my jeans then reached into the pocket of the backpack careful to conceal the money I peeled a twenty dollar bill from the wad. Face stood also and brushed wildly at his clothes. I handed him the money and at first he acted reluctant to receive it; hesitant. I pushed it at his outstretched hand. I then heel to toe removed my converse "Dr. J" style red and white tennis kicking them across to him. Suddenly for a second that anger returned to his face. "Take'em Face. Please." I implored quietly. He picked them up after taking a firm hold of the bill then walked back toward the abandoned house. I stood there looking at it seeing within its windows flickers of light that reminded me of his lighter flaming up. Then there was rumbling and once again the silence of night. As I turned to walk away he called out to me again this time less menacing than when we first met.

"Thanx nigga'! You saved my life tonight bro'. Keep it real Los. I'll see you on the other side."

Life out of Darkness

While sitting and typing these experiences, replaying taped memories of my less than ordinary life; delving into incidents I purposely chose to lock deeply away inside my being, I realized just how sordid my life truly was back then. Many that know me today scarcely believe or can even conceive I was such a dangerously out of control person. And I use that word carefully because during those times in my life I was hardly a person at all.

See, like every great empire that took it upon itself to change the world by imposing its morals of living upon the masses it desired to conquer, there came its inevitable rise and supremely horrendous fall.

So I fight against myself to see just where do I get the nerve to be open and honest about these things that will be appalling to some, disgrace other's, and place my life in the hands of the masses to deem me as they so choose. Many will call me an animal. Many will believe there can never be redemption for such a sinner as me.

Some will declare, how dare I even contemplate finding some eerie kind of solace from the stories I write from the very pages of my life? They may even go as far as damning me to hell for being so brazen as to expect that anyone understand my struggles to be free.

But this is..... for all intent and purpose, my redemption song, a melody of weighted orchestrated tones; easy notes to follow; sounds so froth with uneasiness and thunderous claps of disdain, pain, turmoil and peace. It's funny how it sounds plopping aimlessly from my lips. Peace. The word stands alone like the many unethical tribulations and beats of my greatest symphony; untamed.

Because it is here, right here in every single word, the answer I have sought my life to find. I have to see that through the darkness life shines, no matter that it was so harsh even unforgiving. It is what I have become today as a man that allows me to hold my head up high and live today without shame.

And to everyone that reads these stories, everyone under the sound of my voice, hear me roar like a ferocious beast in the wilderness, starving for life; for understanding; for liberty from the prison of the mind.

Take what you will. And leave the rest. We only live once! We only get one shot at this thing called life, so make the best of it because we never know when it will be gone!

........Peace

Optimal Resolution

The depth of my conversion, brimming with mediocrity, fluid while embracing cowardice calamity, is far more demanding than merely conforming to societal existing; the very essence of purpose lost in the "whys and how's". I strive to find reasoning, but is there truly a reason to be sought?

The rivers of life; flowing like rushing tidewater; swirling and churning deep undertow sucking down my aura, such that I appear old and worn. However, the grandiose ones cheerfully demand I keep my head up. Find a way out of the dismal abyss where pity comfort's my being. They taunt me. Exclaiming, "You've changed so much!" So why do I itch to bash their mouths?! Pummel my hardship, toil and strife into the very well sown blanket of their life.

But I have changed. Maybe not for the best, yet I am better. I can awaken each day disregarding the pain that envelopes my body, ignoring my circumstance from dealing carelessly with fate. I give honor to God and praise Him for showing me mercy nevertheless. I thank Him for blessing me with the breath of life just one more day. No matter that the dread of my past is ever present before me. Each time I look in the mirror or see my doctor for lab work, it is there, but I live. I once tried to hide my aging by cutting the gray hairs that spring up more rapidly now that I am older, now I proudly display them like a badge of honor. They represent life to me.

Some have called me foolish because I still believe in a place called "hope". It is a place where optimism and persistence build a bridge across the divide of despair to a land where dreams come true. It is in this place where we are allowed to think about tomorrow even though it isn't promised to come, where we live in the here and now, diligently seeking that which affords us productivity, equality and abundant life. Thus my conversion takes form inside my heart. It encases my life as a tailored made glove fit's a hand. I am a man and nothing past, present or future can take this fact away.

Lord I thank you, for allowing me to see many days. It is by Your mercy, it is by Your grace! I thank you for lifting me from the waters of turmoil that were drowning me. I thank You for rescuing me. I thank You for what You've done for me and the things You are yet to do. I thank You for my life, my health and my strength! I thank You Lord for dying for my sins that I should not have to be burdened by what I have done. I thank You for forgiving me even though I know You are there and I still tend to waiver and doubt. I know if it wasn't for Your love I would long ago be dead sleeping in a grave but You have seen fit that I live on and for THIS, I THANK YOU!

And joy returns to my heart. If only for right now.... I am happy.

Freedom 2

"Have we forgotten that once we were brought here, we were robbed of our name, robbed of our language? We lost our religion, our culture, our GOD! And now, many of us, by the way we act, have even lost our minds...." Orator unknown

It's a shame that we deem this fight to be against "The Man" a societal epithet for social indignity. But I ask you, why are we killing each other on the streets? What man is killing another man of the same ethnicity because the colors that one wears is either blue or red?! What man is standing on street corners selling crack to his own mother, brother, sister, daughter and son? What will it take for us to realize that we are only hurting ourselves?! What my people, will it take for us to see the damage we're doing every time another dropout, another gang or drug related murder; another act of ignorance perpetrated against the very race to which we swear to belong happens? Why are we killing ourselves? Why are we doing this? What point is there to prove through annihilation of our own doing?

This is not to incite the kind of hatred that leads to rebellion against the established laws of our land. Instead we are to rebel against the insanity we are causing against our race! It is past time for the black family to unite!! It is time for us to fight against our own ways of thinking and living! It is time for us to strive for education rather than extinction! It is time for us to pull up our pants, rid our minds of the derogatory language we speak to one another! It is time, black people, for us to take a stand for what is right and to seek to attain that which will restore the dignity set down by our forefathers! Let us, through our actions, gain the trust of the communities where we live! We MUST instill the integrity of productive, responsible members of this society. But first we MUST restore the integrity of our communities! We MUST fight for freedom!

The kind of freedom that is given to us because we have earned it; the right to stand proud and unshakable in the face of adversity is what we must fight for. We should earn, through our civility, the right as set down by the constitution to go wherever we want and not be looked down upon or frowned at. We can say what we want through the reasonable knowledge we gain to back it up! We can live as the free people we are supposed to be because we've proven that we deserve this.

We MUST stop wasting our lives and the lives of future generations. We MUST as a people stop the madness before there is no future for us to uphold."

(Freedom is directed to anybody that lives with the bondage of ignorance, abuses, or indignity that plagues our human race)

Freedom 1

"Can we assert then that those of us who have thoroughly been bound will ever come to understand and believe in freedom? That without experiencing a daily spiritual growth as that of a baby experiencing life for the first time, even though for some of us age would imply adulthood, still we awake each morning implicating that a substantial re-birth has occurred.

Freedom for us "We the people of these United States of America in order to form a more perfect union...." should mean that we are charged to actively become an omnipresence in our family's, children's, and communities' fight for freedom. Look around you. Our futures are being decimated by abuses, drug and alcohol, sexual and physical abuses that are setting the stage for bondage and giving them the mindset that all is lost. They ask," What is there to do right for? What do I have to look forward to?" and our response is to sit idly by and bury lives along with unfulfilled hopes....... Freedom.

Let us attempt to form bonds with one another that shall tear apart social injustice and racial ignorance. Let our goal be to seek courage out of shame, guilt and distrust. May this courage be the power that fuels our capacity, as well as others, so that our efforts will support a desire to be free in every aspect of our lives, as living examples. For without freedom we and our future generations of promise shall only.......everyone, live as slaves."

A King has Died (When kings die)

The family was burying the second cousin killed in the course of one month. I sat there looking around at all the people, some wailing, some lamenting loudly, some just out of control with grief. The choir dressed in purple robes humming a woeful tune while the pastor prayed for an end to the violence that captured the city and its youth. I just sat there in awe with no feelings of sadness because my anger and tendency for revenge overshadowed any emotion. Then a slight nudge from my mother sitting next to me brought me crashing back to what was going on in the sanctuary of the church where death loomed seeking its next victim. I was lead by an usher to the podium then left there alone. I fumbled inside the pockets of the dress jacket I wore until I found the piece of paper upon which I had prepared these words........

"Lay gallant and peaceful. For no more designer clothes or fine jewelry shall be your shield. Now only wood encased in the finest marble rock, a tomb for the dead body once known to all as a king. Looking now, down on his lifeless form, mourners or should we all be truly called by lesser standards "browsers", walking slowly by with an uncanny sadness in our eyes, trying to show remorse with thankless gleams of gladness that it isn't us laying there. And still we wonder....If it were who would be looking down on us?
But here lies a king, one of thousands that lived ferociously, concerned, yet fearlessly, motionlessly waiting to be finally laid to rest for all eternity. This king, careful, quick but slow enough to see all around; too slow to see what was closest; too fast to have realized not a single person or thing in that world where he reigned cared. And now, these last words spoken by me, not sure if everyone here respected or admired my cousin as I had come to, because no matter our choices we were still family. Even so my words are soft and carefully chosen because there are those that will never understand. I'm just hoping to say something right."

After the long procession from the church we came to the burial grounds. Lowering the casket into the deep chasm where it will after being filled with dirt protect my cousin from harm evermore. And the kingdom lives on as the king; our king is laid to rest.

No Name

"....His eye is on the sparrow.... and I know He watches me..."

It was a regular night of hustle and bustle on "crack avenue",
late June temperature, stillness in the air, a lot of traffic cascading
to and fro either by foot or car; people were busy being served the
chemical myself and several others sold in tiny plastic bags.
"Crack" in all its euphoria inducing esteem was being peddled that
night to the many users frequenting the block. I stood at my usual
corner and dealt primarily with usual customers. But the feel
wasn't right. It was like waiting for the police to come and whisk
me away but their visual presence wasn't one to put any of us
dealers on alert. Just waiting for the inevitable is how I felt. My
bodyguard and I were smoking a blunt (weed wrapped in a cigar
paper) when a very familiar face approached. It was "CB". He used
to sell crack but now he was just another customer. He neared
where we stood slowly kind of apprehensive, like he was afraid.
But at the time I had come to affiliate that type of approach as
someone with no money trying to think of how they would get a
hit from me for free. Being a street dealer afforded me to become a
very good perceiver of people. Their reactions and body
movements helped me to discern things about behaviors and
attitudes so I could better handle situations that arose at any given
time. That is a plus on the streets. It can save you from being
robbed or worse. This night it would save my life. CB now stood a
couple of feet in front of me but he was staring at my bodyguard.
We all knew each other and never had a harsh word spoken to or
about one another. In fact it was CB whom used to "school" me on
things he'd learned from "Old Hats" the old dealers that trained
him in the street etiquette on how to deal successfully. He and I
were good friends until he became a user, now we barely spoke
even though we saw each other daily. I chalked it up to a pride
thing.

"Wats up Silas?" he asked my bodyguard. There was sullenness in his voice that put me on edge. I just looked at him from where I stood, not saying a word or acting involved in their conversation.

"Nuthin' CB, wat's up with you?" Silas retorted.

   Silas had a voice that matched his persona exactly, being 6'5", 225 pounds of brooding muscular man. Silas and I had met a couple of years earlier the day he was released from prison. He needed a job and I was fortunate enough to have a position open. I took him in giving him a place to stay, shopped for him some clothes and supported his habit. He was a crack user, but he was a different kind. He would smoke but he wasn't a "baser" like those that did whatever they had to in order to get high. I liked that about him. He always maintained an air of assuredness about himself even when stoned he never lost his train of thought. CB moved closer to Silas. The two stood there momentarily like two sumo wrestlers feeling the other out. Where would be the best place to strike that first blow?

"Man y'all got any "rocks"?" CB asked, sounding now desperate for the answer to be "yes". CB had his hands in his pant pockets which Silas never let anyone close to us in a posture like that. It was common practice to always keep their hands visible at all times. However CB was different. He wasn't a threat. But everyone is a threat on crack streets; everyone. I now walked over closer to CB and said,

"CB, what you good for?" It was my way of asking how much crack he wanted to purchase.

"Los, man wat's up!? It's your boy CB! How's it goin'? Slow tonight hunh?" he replied. I know exactly who he is and that it wasn't slow. A wrong answer to the second question could mean giving a tester hit; we both know this matter of factly.

"Yeah CB it's slow as turtles tonight man." I said with a smirk. For some reason, I began to get antsy and this annoyed me, slight of anger.

"Man. Los, tell your boy to stand down! Damn it's me nigga! Y'all niggas done got all blown up and shit! Nigga ain't nobody here for that shit!" He took it to the next level for me.

"Ain't nobody doin' nothin' CB. We just hustlin'," I said still hiding my disdain with calm. That's me. I would always be a masker, one that hid expression well. Talking like nothing was wrong or about to happen when I was about to smash someone's head in.

"Los, I need a wake up man. Somethin' to get me started. I promise to bring you some paper if you can do that for me." CB finally got around to telling his purpose. I always respected when a baser would just be honest about what they want rather than take me through changes about this shit. I looked at Silas and he nodded a resounding yes. Partly because he knew this would get him a quick hit also. I looked away but Silas knew what this meant so he went to the phone booth where we stashed our product and retrieved the crumpled paper bag that inconspicuously hid the crack we sold. He came back and gave it to me. I then pulled out a specially made bag of "cut" this was the dust of bigger rocks that I would give samples from or to those regulars having no more money and wanting a hit. I shook two pebble sized pieces into my hand then resealed the bag and handed it back to Silas. He walked it to the phone booth then motioned for CB to meet him and they both sat in an abandoned car a few feet away from me. It was dark so soon as one struck a lighter the flame burst illuminated the darkness of the car. I thought, "no wonder they get arrested for possession. a cop can see this from a mile away." After a couple minutes Silas returned to his post. His eyes always got bigger after a hit. He would be a little fidgety, but he was ready for anything that would come up. CB then came hurriedly over to where I stood and Silas immediately cut his path and closeness by standing in CB's path.

"LOS! Tell yo' boy to stand down nigga'!" CB demanded, trying to peer around Silas to get a look at me.

"That's it CB. No more freebies till you bring some paper." I said with no hesitation.

"Los, that's some good shit man! Let me get some work nigga'! You know I can sell that shit!" There was urgency in his voice. I just looked at CB. Damn. This used to be the "man" around here for so long. He used to always dress in the latest fashions. Wear gold chains and rings. Drive a bomb ass car. Now..... he is standing there pulling a dope fiend move asking me to give him some crack to sell when we both know all he will do is smoke it all. He is wearing blue jeans that have huge holes in the knees. His clothes are dirty and he smells like he hasn't bathed in weeks; his eyes wide and concentrated. Lips moving bizarrely even when he wasn't talking they would be pursing and flinching about.

"Nah CB. I can't give no work right now." I said and like a flood gate had been opened for him to exude his anger CB ranted.

"FUCK YOU NIGGA'! YOU AIN'T 10 FEET TALL NIGGA'! YOU AIN'T SHIT LOS! THINK A NIGGA' CAN'T TOUCH YO' ASS BITCH?! I TAKE ALL YO' SHIT NIGGA'! YOU KNOW ME NIGGA'! THINKIN' CAUSE I SMOKE I DONE GOT WEAK OR SOM'THIN'! NIGGA' I STILL THE BADDEST NIGGA' ROUND HERE LOS!" CB was pacing back and forth with Silas directly in front of him.

I listened, but Silas had enough of CB's threats and without warning hit CB in the face knocking him out. One freaking punch dropped CB to the ground like a ton of bricks. Silas then looked back at me with this look of surprise! Not surprised that he knocked CB out, we had seen that done to others many times, but maybe because he had to resort to doing this to CB. Silas then picked CB up like he weighed absolutely nothing, and placed his unconscious body on the grassy curb. He looked to me again and I shrugged my shoulders. "He'll be alright." I said. We both stood there peering at CB like he was something exquisite on display. But in my mind I was thinking how I never would end up like that, strung out on crack and my life being that messed up. After a short while CB gained consciousness. He stood there wobbly, brushing his clothes and murmuring something unintelligible. Then like a fire had been lit beneath his feet he shouted.

"Y'ALL NIGGA'S GONNA DIE TONIGHT!!" He then ran off screaming this at the top of his smoked out lungs as he disappeared around the corner. Silas looked at me and we both knew it was time to call it a night at that corner so we got the crack from the phone booth and our pistols from the trunk of the abandoned car and walked in the direction CB had ran. Not that we were following. To us CB was an idle threat one of many we received on a daily basis from some angry crack head at any time we said no to them. After walking four blocks we came up to the hotel where we had a room for the night and there was so much going on in the parking lot people were standing around talking, laughing, smoking. Silas and I looked at each other with huge grins. The place was jumping and meant we could stay off the corner for awhile. Soon as we were noticed people came rushing toward us. "Los, you holdin'?" they asked. I nodded. There were people on the balcony surrounding the second floor rooms. I saw a fellow dealer there and he motioned for me to come up. I gave the crack to Silas and went upstairs. I kept a watchful eye as Silas served people. He really enjoyed having this control I could see it in his eyes and the way he moved about. This is his night to be 10 feet tall. As I leaned against the railing where my associate stood he extended a fist and I gave him pounds with a fist of my own.

"Nigga' tell me you got weight wit' you! Come down here makin' all the loot! Nigga' I gotta get mine too!" he said. His name was "Big Bootsy". He was short, black as coal skin tone, bald head, deep heavy voice like sandpaper, husky sounding, 300 or so pounds at 5'5". A huge man he was and cousin to CB. I told him I didn't have any weight but if he wanted a large package I could take the trip to get it. Before answering, as if suddenly remembering, he said "Nigga' yo boy knocked CB out!?"

"Yeah." I spoke but quietly trying to be compassionate. "He was trippin'. Silas didn't want..."

Big Bootsy cut me off. "That nigga' asked me for a pistol for you! I didn't give him one but he said he gonna kill you tonight nigga', he down at the baser room on the first floor, end room by the entrance." He now looked in the direction where he spoke of and there was CB coming out of the room and walking toward Silas. I didn't see any gun but the way he walked was with attitude and this gave me reason for concern so I rushed downstairs.

"CB!!!", I called out. "Here I am nigga'!!" I shouted.

Silas turned placed the crack in a pant pocket then moved toward CB quickly. But as we both moved in on CB another man came out of the baser room shouting at CB. He was clearly much older than CB and looked a little better in shape.

"Nigga'! YOU THINK YOU GON' JUST TAKE MY MONEY!"

He said with hostility rushing in on CB. The two embraced and rustled back and forth then fell to the ground. A crowd was now gathering as the two rolled on the pavement. Silas stood next to me still pushing people away from getting close to me. Big Bootsy was to my right not helping his cousin or trying to break up the fracas. He was content just to watch as well as everyone else. CB got the upper hand on the old man and stood to his feet. The man then made it up as well and the two stood toe to toe breathing hard from exhaustion. It seemed the way they breathed they had been fighting hard for at least an hour or so but it was only a couple minutes of jostling. The old man told CB he didn't appreciate that CB took his money and wanted CB to either get the crack he was suppose to buy with it or give the money back.

CB looked directly at me then said, "I ain't doin' shit!"

He then pulled a pistol from his pant waist pointed it at the old man and fired. "PHOW!" Everyone scattered except Silas, Big Bootsy and I. CB started yelling, "THATS FOR YOU LOS! YOU THINK I'M A JOKE!? I AIN'T SCARED NIGGA'! I AIN'T SCARED!" The way the old man struck out in a running stride no one knew what had happened. I watched him run in a circle around the parking lot as cars tried to leave the scene. People darted about in and out of rooms. The old man was holding a hand to his throat. That's when I noticed dark wetness oozing between his fingers. He made a complete circle then fell to the pavement just at my feet. Now it was apparent that he had been shot in the neck as blood spewed in a stream from a hole there. I looked to CB, his eyes raging with fright, his lips dancing wildly in a solo pirouette to a song only they could hear. Big Bootsy yelling at him to "RUN!" but CB was frozen there for a second or two, then getting his wit's CB charged off into the dark of an adjoining street. I could tell he had no idea what he had just done. I knelt and took the old mans outstretched arm in my hand. He was gurgling for air through the blood that flowed into his airway. He too had a far off look in his eyes it was like he knew he was going to die and was trying to find someone familiar in his mind. Even though he looked at me I don't believe he knew I was there. And just maybe if he did he was silently asking me to help him stay alive. But no words came from his partially opened mouth. I tried to assure him by holding his hand and telling him, "You gonna' be alright buddy, just hold on," that calm steely reserve of mine taking precedence at this time of panic.

"You're gonna' be alright bro, just hold on."

Then his hand tightened around my own and he died, his eyes still open wide, sweat trickling over his face as blood seeped from the wound in his throat. It was somber in meaning, him dying like that. I didn't know what to do or how to do anything to save him. I just knelt there holding his hand staring at his lifeless form. I looked for signs of life, like he really wasn't dead just resting. As life's blood now emptied to the ground and puss laden fluid drained through air bubbles forming an abstract pattern beneath his head, I hoped he would begin to move again. Silas' hand rested on my shoulder bringing me back from where the old man and I had found rest together. I looked up at him and he said, "Man we better go," nothing more just a command. But I couldn't go anywhere. I could not move from the spot or release my hold of the old mans hand.

"Doe's anybody know him?" I asked.

Silas, itchy to leave before the police came, shook his head no and then looked around. I did the same. The parking lot that was once full of life was now nearly empty. People stood in doorways peeking out at the scene. A girl we knew who was in the baser room stood a couple feet behind us. She chimed in, "Nobody know his name. He just called "Pops" by everyone here." her remark was soft and soothing, not like the normal based out drones common place for a smoker. "Pops.", I thought.

"Damn. Nobody knows his name."

I eventually sent Silas to our room and waited with the old man until the paramedics arrived. It didn't take them long to come. The motel was frequented by them daily, either because someone was found by housekeeping after an overdose, or someone had been beaten up in a fight over crack. They were there within 10 minutes but it took the police close to 2 hours to arrive. And once they did the old man still lay there on the cold unforgiving pavement for hours through the misty cool of late night into the frosty dew of early morning he lay there. The spot where his blood formed a puddle beneath him, the same blood that glimmered earlier was now a dried, black spot..........Damn. Nobody knew his name.

Several months had passed since that night. Silas and I were still doing what we called "good business". No one talked about the old man or the events of that night. That was the code of the streets. It was just one of those things that happened and everybody was glad it didn't happen to them. No one knew for sure whatever became of CB. But rumors are what spread after events like that. So some said he had been captured and arrested in Mississippi and was awaiting transport. Some said he was living with family in North Carolina.

November 1996...... Years later. Wow it all seems so uncanny that the same streets where I and Silas sold crack rocks and fought and played were now where we scrounged for crack hits ourselves. The same motel where the old man was killed was not my place of rest anymore, but the baser room was where I went to smoke now. It was second nature for me to hustle to get money, only now it wasn't for paying my bills and buying me and Silas nice things. Every penny I got belonged to a dealer to pay off debts for crack given in advance of the money, and if I had anything left over I spent it on crack also. I was smoking heavy and no longer had a nice apartment. I slept in abandoned houses; on the very same streets where I once sold rocks I now scrambled to survive. I would go for days without eating, bathing or sleeping just like CB used to do. I would pull those same crack stunts as CB tried on me to get high; that behavior, which I so detested was now my way of life. And on that November day as I was arrested and being taken to the county jail for attempted murder of an law enforcement officer. As the transport vehicle passed the motel parking lot. I sadly looked there and saw the old man lying on the pavement. I went to jail and found out CB had been caught and awaited trial for the old man's murder. When he found out I had been locked up CB had his attorney subpoena me to court on his behalf. I didn't want to do it because my own dilemma far outweighed the old man's murder. But God saw things differently and I went to deposition hearing and told the truth of that fateful night. I never found out the old mans name...... but at least he and his family could find closure. In some strange way we all found closure. I was sentenced to 90 years in prison. CB was sentenced to 10 years.

Ghetto Blessings: Understanding

This may very well be the greatest piece I could ever compose. It is not eloquent, nor sweet. These words I pray in all sincerity.... for someone, will allow them through me an opportunity to experience a freedom I could not. This is not a bitter protest of the life I lived. By God, this is far from an attempt to gain sympathy by pitying one's intellect out of discorded prose. I am albeit an angelic being full of serenity. No matter misdeeds and committed sins. Read if you will and open your heart to absorb meaning. Let this sink in so deeply that out of non - sense, there maybe found a semblance of the love we all harbor and protect so vehemently. Let this be the key that unlocks what we have imprisoned within our souls and desperately cries out for release.

I may not ever know what it is to be unbound spiritually. I may never know what it is to forgive. Happiness so sought after, that has eluded me continuously. No contentment have I found. I write this not only for you. It is done primarily for anyone including myself needing understanding. We all define confusion as not being able to understand, even if this understanding details the simplest ingredient of life. A life complicated by emotions, failures, triumphs, people, places...... and time. Please believe this is not to say I have never been happy although I truly can't remember what happiness entails. Fleeting, barely noticeable out of all the turmoil and self – destruction, I hide furiously behind a fragile mask of testosterone and pride. Here in the silence of words written, lies the melody of a song manifested to fit a voice in our mind of someone we long to hear speak them aloud. Sadness, joy, pleasure and fear; smiles gracing lips we long to kiss; laughter we long to hear and love we yearn to feel.

Life comes to everyone only once. A beating heart; functioning bodies of human ability and where does it go after death? Someone once said to me "every headstone has etched into it a birth date. There is a slash. Then date of death. Its not when we were born or died that anyone really remembers. However the slash, what we did in between. The life we lived after being born until we die, that's what they remember most". So I ask, "How will you be remembered?". I have thus far no crowning achievements. Nothing to state that will give me honor among people memorialized throughout history. I never mediated any marches. I never stood before a crowd to orate a stirring speech for change. I am lowly in stature. The meaning of heroism implicates that I have been a coward. Inside I cry so many tears that it has become too much of a task fighting against crying outwardly. If there are no visible tears, the frowns and looks of disdain scar my already chiseled face.

Woe the weary traveler, many miles ventured, looking for something which to him can not be found. Perseverance falters. Exhaustion overcomes strength. I have fallen and risen ingloriously. Prayed and begged determinedly. I have struggled to maintain sanity when all that prevailed was chaos. And now my only desire is to pen this...... my greatest symphony.

Ghetto Blessings is a compilation of events that shaped my life. I began writing this over 30 years ago while serving a 9 month jail sentence. Back then being incarcerated was the only time I found to write. Not that I wanted to be locked up, just that outside the institutional barrier my life activities afforded me no time. The purpose of Ghetto Blessings had nothing to do with gratefulness in the early days of its conception. Most who read the stories did not read for meaning but rather to escape the long, timeless days of incarceration. Over the years as each event took on varying faces, different states, different institutions, Ghetto Blessings began to take on a far more extravagant meaning. Maybe not to those that read but certainly to me. There became a noticeable pattern of misdeeds, incarcerations, releases, struggles and even blessings in my life. I began to realize I would gain so much only to throw it all away, time and time again; that out of all the violence I would be spared, maybe not from physical, emotional, and spiritual pain, but definitely from death. After all I had been through the blessings didn't become evident until 2006 when I spoke before a group of 17 juvenile delinquent teenagers at a facility for wayward teens. I was suppose to be talking about the ills of drug and alcohol abuse but what God brought out of me that day was a testimony of His mercy and love constructed from a broken mans life.

It is my belief that every living human being commands a defining moment in their life when they make a difference. Ghetto Blessings isn't to magnify the epic endeavors of my life. It isn't to find glorification out of misdeed. This however is truly written to represent the small seemingly insignificant graces bestowed along the way; graces that saved me from death countless times. See, by all intent and purpose I should be dead but God has and continues to watch over me. Even when I have doubted; even as I witness the evil that people are prone to act out; the senseless scenes of violence in the world; wars, homelessness, and starvation; the over crowded prisons and teenage illiteracy and delinquency, I am forever grateful. I am spared from the eternal pit of spiritual damnation and given this, through these words........ my finest masterpiece; a symposium of gratitude. I realize today that some of us have to go through defeat to truly understand victory. Some have to experience death to truly live. I had to pen this in its entirety in order for me to see the workings of a power far greater than any in this world. My eyes had to be opened by reliving my life less ordinary, so that I can finally see beyond the superficial and look deeper into the spiritual aspect of living. Therein lays the blessing. Not being killed or so afflicted even though stricken with a terminal illness I still have meaning. I still live through affliction and with circumstance to purpose a greater constitution of life!

I could easily say, " If I had paid heed to Ma Johnson or the "old man" then the things that transpired in my life would never have taken place". But then again I have to recognize everything happened as it was suppose to. Understand, God to me is the author and director of this movie titled "My Life" and I am the leading actor; a devious egotistical mass of masculinity so arrogant that I refused to adhere to or follow His direction. Until now at Oscar presentation time I would receive best supporting actor awards for characters portrayed in this movie written expressly for me. I am right now, at this very point of my life striving for something vastly greater. It is my wish though I may not garner such accolades in this earthen vessel, I wish to one day stand before God in the spirit and hear Him say, "Well done My good and faithful servant. You are My child in whom I am well pleased." thus on that day I shall receive my Oscar. On that day I shall finally be set totally free. Until then, I will keep moving onward. No matter what may come up against me I shall trudge on. No matter that storms will rise up over me, I shall not be moved. I will awaken each morning with thanksgiving for being allowed to see another day. I will praise God for saving me from an untimely death and ask that He watch over me as I go through each day I am given. I will learn to thank Him for my ups and downs, and for putting people in my life that believe in me when I can't find it to believe in myself. Finding joy out of sadness, health and strength out of pain and weakness, my heart will continuously adore Him for through it all He still loves me enough to keep giving me another chance to find redemption.

The Old Man and Me

I met an old man one day while I stood on a street corner wasting my life away. I looked at him as he slowly hobbled toward me, a cane in one hand for support. It steadied him and kept him from falling over while aiding him to walk. There was still a hint of discomfort in his facial expression. To him the cane gave him strength but to me it was a reminder of old age and weakness. As he approached I looked at his eyes, narrow and beaming they were. After closer observation they too were staring intently back at me.

"What you starin' at old man?" I said from nervousness, hoping he would just look away. Instead he answered softly with disappointment sounding in his voice.

"Nothing much...... I look at you and see nothing much at all."

I looked away now. Down the long, empty block. It was my neighborhood. Broken down houses lined both sides of the street abandoned to fend for themselves like many that dwell here. Not many people were out that day just a few children playing tag; a couple were standing at a bus stop waiting and talking. An old woman was raking leaves from her front yard of patchy grass and dusty, red dirt. The old man was now standing next to me. Just staring at me even though I refused to give him direct eye contact I sensed he was. I could feel his eyes on me and I felt uncomfortable so I was about to walk away when he spoke.

"Boy, what you doing? Just standing here?" He asked tapping the back of my leg with the cane. I flinched but didn't respond.

"Was it that I called you "Boy" that make you feel disrespected by me enough not to answer? Or is it that you don't know why you standing here doing nothing with your life son?" His voice crackled and even though it sounded strong age had taken away its power.

"Well if you're mad because I called you "boy", how come you ain't mad when so - called friends call you worse things than that!? I maybe old but I still hear very well. You young bucks calling each other "nigga'" like its something honorable. Something powerful! When the word is derogatory! It means stingy, petty and annoying. A demeaning term used to describe black people....." he said, "Why don't you look at me boy? Afraid you might see some truth?" he stood there waiting for a response.

"I don't know old man." I snorted.

"Well you know I'm old! And you know I'm a man! That's what you keep calling me."

"Why you even talkin' to me old man!?" I asked hoping I would anger him to just walk on. Instead he took it as a cue to continue.

"Maybe you need talking to boy?"

"If I needed that I would get it at home from my mom!" I snapped.

"Maybe.... but also maybe you need Listening."

He sat down on a bench there. I looked at him with a sideways glance and he motioned with a frail, wrinkled hand for me to come and sit beside him. I don't know why but something pushed me to go and sit. So I did. He then rested his cane on the ground and held out his hand to me.

"My name is Elijah Freedom Wilson." He stated proudly.

We sat silent for a moment then he huffed and like a great orator standing before the pulpit of thousands of waiting listeners he began to talk..... Only it was just he and I.

"I grew up here boy. These very streets I once played on, worked on, and wasted lots of time trying to survive. Just like you doing right now. I remember like it was yesterday the night we children played hide and seek and that night I met my future wife, Sadie. Of course we didn't know it then", he giggled and suddenly hid face lit up to reveal very bright white teeth.

"Yeah, us young ones were always out here running, yelling, playing. Then we all grew a little older and had to get jobs. Some of us shined shoes. Some bagged groceries. Some delivered newspapers. Me, I went cross town with my mother to clean white folks houses. From the time we entered till the time we left I felt so inferior. Do you know what that word means boy?"

I didn't answer.

"Well it means "less than someone or something else in stature and dignity." He answered his own question. We both sat there not saying a word. I think he wanted me to say something but there was nothing I could say at that point.

"So I said to my mother one day, "momma' I'm not going to work up there no more. I hate the way them people look at and talk to us. We have to clean their mess and raise their children!" ; you know what boy, she cried and said, "You don't have to go no more Freedom. But you got to work." I said "fine" and started looking for a job. Well it was during the Great Depression of nineteen - thirty two", he said matter of fact like with no hesitation.

Then his eyes opened a little wider as if he was looking to see the times had changed back to what they were for him then. He looked up and down the street.

"During the Great Depression wasn't no real jobs to be had. Most of the factories and stores had close because everybody was poor. So the only work for us black folk was shining shoes or cleaning houses and stuff like that. I made up my mind I wasn't catering to no man so I started hustling the streets. Selling whiskey and being a doorman at after hour joints around the city. Yeah...., I was a true hustler! At least that's what I thought....." he paused and now all the wideness of his eyes disappeared and the narrow tight slits returned. His face frowned awkwardly.

"Everything was going good. That's what making that fast money wants you to believe, that life is good when really life is passing you by. I married Sadie and we had a baby girl, Lola." His words became soft again but this time spoken with a deep affection. The old mans expression changed to sadness.

"It was then my momma passed of the cholera. Not long after that, a few years too soon Sadie passed then Lola right behind her......"

A lonely tear rolled down his cheek. He bowed his head then with every ounce of energy he could gather. I could tell this because he took a very deep inhaled breath. His fingers strained into a tightly made fist, he jutted his chest out and looked me straight in the eyes.

"I got arrested for hustling whiskey and they sent me to prison for the next 20 years of my life. When I got out, the whole world had changed. I didn't know anybody because most of my friends were either dead or locked up. I didn't have no trade because all I ever did was hustle the streets so I couldn't get a job."

He stopped exhaling hard and long then picked up the cane. He shakily struggled to stand but he made it. He gently placed his free hand on my head and this time I did not twitch.

"You don't have to lose your life in these streets son. Go to school get an education. Learn a trade and gain all that life has to offer. You hear me son?"

I heard him loud and clear but didn't want to understand what he said until years later and I have been to prison. Now I know that life is a precious gift God gives us to grow and experience. But it is up to us which way we will explore. And though many of us will make mistakes it is never too late to correct them but the best thing to do is travel the right paths in the first place.

50

The Prodigal Son

...... And in his later years, when he had no one else to turn to that could help him change his life, he turned to God. But the change wasn't instantaneous. There was no bright light that shone upon him or angels speaking parables of a great coming. He didn't even talk to God personally. He had lived his life by his rules. For years he'd done as he pleased and now he felt in his spirit a higher calling if you will; something that ate at him. He knew he had to live under a different authority. One morning he woke up and realized it is by Gods grace, mercy, and forgiveness that he has lived this long. That all his trials and tribulations were of Gods stern chastisement because he knew God and still ignored Gods will.

Now it is apparent that with age all those talents he was given and never utilized are slowly becoming passing memories. God has found use for them in someone more deserving. Still he fights to utilize what he can or is able to. No matter how useless his conscience leads him to believe they are.

And now he prays for the chance to make the last years, minutes, days, seconds of his life.... "right". Right by all those people who ever knew him and even to those who don't. Right by his biological heritage that only got to see him one way. All the bad he did is what they remember most. So he seeks to show them the greatness God so ordained for him to possess. Now he prays for closeness and love. He prays for salvation out of the misery the life he upheld plagued his soul with. He strives for respect and dignity so that when his time comes he may die with integrity and leave those behind much better off then when he was here.

If I don't wake up......

There is a recurring nightmare. Maybe it wouldn't be so frightening if it didn't actually happen and all the scenes were my imagination through dream sequences. Maybe if I had done something different then no one would have died that night and I wouldn't have to carry this image in my soul. As I sit here now, wow, that very night, which I feel in my being as if I have to relive it in order to survive. But deeper still I am damned to, even in my sleep, because in some ways I seek forgiveness; in others it is my way of saying thanks.

My cousin and I attended a party on the wrong side of town that June night. Damn it was hot! By this time the Southside Boys family of dealers and thugs had grown to immense proportions. I had honestly begun a slow descent away from reality into a dark world where life is feeble and death a welcome ally. I had a target on me, constant cross hairs followed my every move. Police investigators were piecing together the puzzle of my involvement. Other gangs were plotting a vicious and bloody take over, while in my own ranks there was a plan to oust me as violently as possible. My target was one to set an example to everyone else brave enough to wear their own. Still I ignored my intuition. This was a party I had to make my presence felt at. There was no way around it. Needless to say, I was there as more than an ignorant man unafraid of the death that loomed over me like a vulture waiting for its prey to finally cease moving. I was there because I didn't want those in my world to see that deep inside I was a coward. That's what it meant to me. Fearless. Ha! The party was being hosted by members from a rival gang. Members we thought to have taken out a hit on one of our own family just months before. This was to be our show of authority and fearlessness. In the minds of every Southsider we owned every street, alley, house, project and person in the city. There was no DOUBT we were there strictly for trouble and dared anyone to "fuck" with us, my cousin carrying a loaded .44 magnum revolver and myself a .9mm semi - automatic. There was no other member with us. No one else thought it to be a good idea for such brazen attitude. Those who were truly "family" the ones I could honestly say would go down in battle with and for me cautioned against making such a potent statement without a show of numbers. Those who conspired against me could care less. My cousin was one who just cared about me his "true" family. Now I wonder how much did I care about him?

The party was held inside the confines of a three bedroom apartment. By the time we arrived the place was well pass capacity limits and people spilled into the hallway, down the stairs and into the street. Of course not everyone there was an enemy. There were business associates that needed the product we sold. There were potential members and women that wanted to be down with the hottest family in the city. Although they were there... that still didn't mean enough to deter the events that had to take place.

The nightmare takes off from that point..... as if it was right now even though years have passed. I am dancing with a female I came to know as "Penny". We are entangled in a sensual mix of open sexuality and gyrating movements that had excited me but had not eased my feeling something bad was about to happen so I kept a stern awareness to everything going on around me. I think that's what bothers me most now. At some point my cousin came up to me while Penny and I danced and kissed. He pulled me close because the music pounded so loud I couldn't hear him unless his mouth was right to my ear. He took my hand at the same time giving me his revolver. My cousin never went anywhere without that gun. Never. I knew this yet I took it from his hand shaking my head trying to make sense of what he was saying. Something about "meeting a female in the parking lot.... get my dick sucked... got a sell... be right back bro'...". Fate is what some would call it. Misfortune. I call it neglect. I watched the back of his head as he meandered through the crowd then vanished through a slim beam of light that appeared as he opened the door then closed it behind him. "AAAAIIIIYYYYEEEEEE!" Seconds turn into hours. Then flash back to the very moment. "COME QUICK! THE GUY YOU ARE WITH.....". I bolt through the crowd, open the door and all the people that lined the hallway are now down at the bottom of the steps mingled in with those that were in the street. I fight through the crowd. No room to move just push forward; Penny right behind, lightly touching my back. I felt her fear. I wonder if she felt mine. I can feel every single eye burning my flesh. The sobs of the scared echoing in my mind like the pumping beat of a headache.; sweat trickling down my face hiding the tears from the pain I have in my gut knotted and wrenching. My cousin, laying there gargling blood from his gasping mouth; rivers of blackish red blood flowing from his nostrils; his hands clutched into painful fist; body trembling; his left leg twitching as if it were totally separated from the rest of his body. All alone it twitched; just like I felt.

"Oh God Please.... please stop this from happening."

I kneel beside him not knowing what to do. What do I do!? The heaving and impulses of life were oozing from him; those eyes that wandered about looking at all this just one last time. "YOU BETTER GET YO' ASS FAR FROM HERE WHILE YOU CAN BITCH!!; NOW MUTHA'FUCKA!!." POP!POP!POP!POP!POP!POP! "GET THE FUCK OUTTA' DODGE BITCH!!!". I drive wildly through traffic, Penny shouting at me to slow down. "Baby please, just slow down." Screeching to a halt at the side of the road and vomiting my intestines into severe cramps of dry heaves; the tears that I can't stop from falling; my clothes stained with his blood; my hands sticky and dark crimson, cramping, shaking violently from anger and fear. She tries to console me but I shun her away with violent outburst of fitful shouts at God and Satan. My pager sounds. "911".... "911". It's strange, how in my dreams there is never any sound.

I still to this day have the exact same nightmare. Nothing ever changes. It is exactly as it was then. Nothing ever changes. I wake up balled into a knot of perspiring flesh, body temperature soaring, head throbbing, tears cascading uncontrollably. Why don't I dream of the retribution? Why do I wake up from these visions from my life, the ones only God and I know about?

Well.... over the years there is one thing that has changed. When I awaken and finally realize it is just that nightmare. I thank God for it being only that. Yeah. Maybe that's the point of me having it. Not as frequent as earlier years. Every now and then it sneaks in and makes for a miserable nights attempt at sleep. But I must have it at those times when I forget to thank God for life. This life I am afforded only by His grace and mercy to live daily. I do forget sometimes. And that "night - mare" is a horrid reminder and the unending source of my gratitude.

Facing the Truth

Ghetto Blessings is not a cinematic take on my life with role playing stars attempting to win an Oscar for their performance. It is not my forlorn attempt at glorifying the life I lived. I didn't live it because I had to. It was my choice. Why? I wish I knew. But this I do know for certain. There is an overwhelming coincidence. I lived to write this. May God bless those ensnared in lifestyles that put their lives on the brink of destruction. I was so blessed many times. It is my desire that all who have the opportunity to read Ghetto Blessings understand it for the miracle of God it is. I never wanted to acknowledge that God had His hands on me. It just seemed like things happened and I was one of the lucky ones to come out of each situation alive. I thought it to be because I ducked when I was supposed to. Or that I didn't go into battle because I knew better. My train of thought was always on my rationale, God had nothing to do with me or how I lived. If I survived a gun fight it was because I was the better shooter or more prepared for war. When I was beaten to within an inch of my life someone found me and got me to a hospital in time. What I lived then is nothing like what I go through from time to time today. I haven't been involved in that reckless lifestyle of death and unsavoriness for more than 23 years, however, it still has an impact on me today. Everything I lived through after that, the using and running, it all affects me today in so many ways. Ghetto Blessings is meant to be a tool. Every one of us has this million dollar Craftsman toolbox sitting in the garage of our lives. It will sit there gathering dust unless we open it and use the tools it holds inside to help us. Life has no book on how to live it, but life does allow us choices. Making the right ones now will definitely afford us better ones to make later. Doing what is right is an option many should consider before getting entangled in a web of wrongs that may never be corrected. As you read this someone dies. As you read this, someone makes the choice to live. My hope is we all find that God is the only right choice to make. Then the rest of our options will be a lot easier.

A Life Without Dope

   While I was out there using. "Getting high". No one could have convinced me one day I would stop. During those times I couldn't even convince myself. To me there was nothing more important than as Narcotics Anonymous refers to its endeavors, "The getting and using and finding ways and means to get more.... Our whole life was centered on drugs in one form or another..... We lived to use and used (as it seemed) to live.... very simply an addict is a man or woman who's life is controlled by drugs...". That was me; a daily forage into the darkness of addiction. From the time I would open my eyes until the time I went to sleep (sometimes days later), all I could think about was using. I am a hopeless dope addict. Once the ball started rolling downhill there is no stopping it without help or divine intervention. Years did I spend chasing drugs; hurting those that loved me more than I loved myself. Stealing, cheating, robbing, lying, whatever it took to get that one more "hit ". Crack cocaine had a grip on my life that gave me no options other than using, drinking alcohol as a "downer", smoking marijuana to stave off the impulse to use when things were slow. But the force of the chemical is so very overpowering, nothing I could do alleviated the urge to stop using. The many times I would say "I'm done with this shit!" or "I'll quit after this one more hit". But I had become such a desolate person, resorting to homelessness because I had broken the trust of my family and friends and wasn't allowed into their homes. I was sleeping in abandoned buildings that offered little shelter from the elements; eating from trashcans because I had no money for food or too much pride to ask for help from one of the shelters. I did receive food stamps but they were only used one day, once a month as cash for drugs. Then the other 29 days I was left to eat anyway I could. The desiccation of dope took me from a 75,000 - 125,000 a year income to having absolutely nothing. It wasn't overnight that I got that way. No. This was the end result from years of delving deeper into addiction. Then after finding my way back several times by the grace of God, maybe a year later, or maybe only a couple of months I would go right back to the stench of addiction because I thought I could handle it the next time. Or I would just stop fighting for my life by succumbing to using as a means to cope. I found every excuse to use, but none to stop the madness.

The progression of dopes effect on my daily life was one that went from taking years to dismantle my existence to in the end taking only a short period of days to totally absolve me of everything I had worth anything including my soul. Each foray into the culture took me further into an abysmal place where only death and life waged war constantly. In the sub - culture of addiction there is no right or wrong because for me using was the only answer. A hopeless "dope fiend" that was me, not only destroying my life but that of anyone I chose to inflict my pain upon. The innocent man robbed unexpectedly while fueling his car. Scarred. The old woman who's purse I snatched as she nonchalantly caroused through a parking lot to her car, not for one minute thinking such a terrible thing was about to happen to her. Not thinking that she would be dragged kicking and screaming over ragged pavement until the strap of her purse breaks and I run off into oblivion. Scarred. Breaking into my own mother's home; the woman that raised me with morals and dignity; the woman that gave me her all to make sure that I lived comfortably as a child. The same woman that accepted me back time and time again I would steal from; took her entire paycheck once. Leaving her no money to pay any of the bills that would insure we had a roof over our heads and food to eat. Dope told me none of that mattered. No one mattered. The only thing I had to look forward to was getting high, no dreams, no aspirations, nothing but dope, nothing but hurting people and above all killing myself.

I am grateful to such groups as A.A, N.A, C.A and the many treatment facilities that offer people another means of living without dope. But most of all I am grateful to God for allowing me the privilege to survive and make it into one of those places where I was reconnected with my hope. A life without dope! My God!!!! Waking up each morning not having to figure out where the next hit was coming from or when. Not having to sleep on the ground because I can't afford a bed; having food in MY refrigerator to eat at anytime I please. "FREEDOM"! That's it for me! Not having to worry about when I was going to be arrested and sentenced to jail or prison. Oh yeah, it is inevitable in that world. Not looking over my shoulder or stalking about like a crazed animal. I can live as the human being I am created to be. Where, for a time in our relationship, my mother would not allow me in her home anymore. I now can come and go as I please having my own key. People don't look at me from a distance with wariness. They don't cross the street at the mere sight of me coming toward them. I can smile today, laugh, be happy and dope has nothing to do with this beautiful emotion. I would be lying if I said my every single day was all "goody - goody, happy - happy!". There are days when I can't seem to make ends meet; days when I would rather bury my head in the ground rather than face them. Sometimes my life just sucks! But you know what the miracle is? Even those days are far better than any I lived with dope.

A Tear for Tiffany

She was merely 8 years young, so sweet and full of life. Tiny in stature, robust in nature, her smile would light up the darkest heart. Her laugh would cause eruptions of uncontrollable fits of joy from anyone able to bear witness. I would stand on the corner of 10th and Main, selling dreams of a life without worry. A chemical fix to whatever ailed those who frequented using it as a means to cope. She would sometimes be on roller skates gliding shakily up and down the block. Occasionally stopping to ask me for a quarter or to give me a piece of her sunshine filled existence. One day she stopped long enough to ask me, "Mr. Why do you stand here all day? I see you when I go to school and when I come home you are still right here! Why?" So young and naïve, I had no answer. She shrugged her tiny shoulders and skated off.

The day she was killed accidentally during a drive - by shooting that took place between rival gangs bent on destruction. The entire neighborhood mourned. The sun did not shine for days after. The night I returned to that corner I stood where a makeshift memorial of wreaths and teddy bears had been placed; white chalk on the sidewalk outlined her last position. It looked angelic; like she was trying to fly away. There was a stain in the pavement where she bled. No matter how anyone tried that stain could not be removed; a reminder of the life that was taken that day; a life that shown so much promise and innocence; a young girl that would never get to find her earthly good through life. But maybe from death her life would forever be remembered as one of hope and determination.

Today I am thinking about you Tiffany, and to answer your question.... " I was a fool. That's why I stood there all day."

62

Seeking Forgiveness

I often wish I could personally say "I pray that you will forgive me," to many people hurt along the way by my actions.

To the brothers sentenced to death and executed by electrocution for murders committed while acting as soldiers in an army with no other purpose than to strike terror in the lives of people.

To the friend sentenced to 141 years in prison for conspiracy.

To the family of those killed.

To the father never going to see his son or daughter grow up.

To the wife left to fend for her and her children without a husband because he is either locked up or dead.

To the mother hearing from a complete stranger "I'm sorry to inform you that your son was killed".

To the ones that endure a loved ones incarceration faithfully.

To the woman selling her body for one more "hit".

To the son that will never get to play catch with his dad.

To the daughter that will never get to ask her parents "is he right for me?".

To the babies born by no choice of their own with addiction.

I never fathomed the far reaching effects of that life style on our society. It never dawned on me that when a life was taken it not only left behind a mother and father. But cousins, nephews, nieces, aunts, uncles, grand babies, sisters, friends, families, and the communities that deteriorated because drugs caused more impoverished living. The depth of my sorrow travels deep. My pain is everyday. I have to suffer this because I am bearing my cross. My burdens of all the pain I caused others. I know it is all in my past. I know I must move on and let go. But it still doesn't allow me the opportunity to find closure personally, to say to those I feel deserve hearing me say it. "I apologize."

I Am so Blessed

........To have lived so long a sinner; to have fallen on my knees and prayed for God to touch my heart and forgive me... Many times. To ask Him to love me and accept my soul enough to save.

Having people in my life that love me regardless of my past; loving me so much they can't just turn away; people that stand beside me, adore me and encourage me to live for brighter days.

........To know emotions so strong, when I felt such emotions were a lie. To realize my pain, understand the reason for the tears I cried inside.

........To finally smile for joy, even weep for happiness I one time couldn't receive. To have the shackles of sin removed from my being and from all the misery God allowed me to be relieved.

........Lord knows I give my best most times to keep Him in my sight. To hold His hand and be close to Him, keeping faith that everything no matter how bad it seems will one day be alright.

........I still fall sometimes but not as hard as I used to. I still sin sometimes but I can pray today for forgiveness when I do.

........To have God in my life keeping me strong. Guiding me. Giving me hope in each day that comes when to me those days seem so few.

........Now I live with purpose. In my heart there are better things to feel. I am so blessed by Gods grace, mercy and love. Its good to finally believe that such holy things are real.

........Though I may not always show it, each day I open my eyes I give God my praise. I am blessed to stand up in the face of fate and be a man so brave.

........Having God keep moving in my life in a glorious and mighty way. I am so blessed! To be a soldier on the battlefield keeping Satan from being victorious each day.

........I am so blessed to love, have joy, fight through pain, and prevail over times so rough when I could not see any good. To have persevered and to fight hard each moment with everything I've got within me to make my salvation in someone's heart easily understood.

My "Ma"

To many she is known as "Shorty". 4'-11" of pure woman. My mom, or as I affectionately call her "Ma", is not my biological mother but she is the only mother I've become accustomed to having. I may never forget the first time I saw her. She is such a beautiful woman. My dad showed up one day at my grandparents farm with the announcement that she is my new mother! I just looked at her (this is her account of that day), "didn't say a word and scared (her) me to death!". Her skin almond brown. Long, flowing black as night hair. A smile that would light the gloomiest room with love. And a voice that could talk to angels or calm the angriest attitude. I fell in love with her immediately even though months would pass before I actually called her Ma. She tells me that I would say she was my wife or that I wanted to marry her! Funny. Didn't quite grasp the concept of a mother - son relationship. I was her only child and the first grandchild to her parents. I even became a status symbol in that family being privileged to know my great - great grandmother (her first great - great grandchild), and great grandparents (the same first). At first I referred to them all by their names but one day my Ma sat me down and told me they are my new family now and it was alright to call them grandparents in respective appropriateness. So I did and the impact among them was nothing short of elation. Until then my dads parents were the only parental guidance or affection I knew. I don't really remember my dad being that much of a force in my life after he took me from my biological mother at the age of 2. Anyway, my new family took me in as one of their own despite being "step - in laws". There were 4 children born to my grandparents. My Ma, and her three brothers one of which was killed by my grandfather in a car accident where he was playing behind the family car and run over. My grandfather was never the same man after that becoming a fearful alcoholic. And thus was my introduction through them to alcoholism and its effects.

They all adopted me as their own flesh and blood is the thing. But my Ma went above and beyond loving me. To this day I never questioned why she never had another child. I just take for granted she couldn't. But the way she spoiled me would have been hard for me to accept another sharing her love. In the early years we spent a lot of time together. She was the only friend I knew or wanted to hang with. We were inseparable. I found comfort in her and this newness of family. I soon moved to a new place with her and my dad so was further thrust into a new environment. And just having her with me made everything alright and less frightening. She took up right where my dads parents left off. Getting me involved in church, school and family responsibility. I would get a 5.00 a week allowance. I sang in the church choir and became an honor roll student. She interested me with writing and sports. Spoiled me with toys. Whatever she could to show her love. I don't remember exactly the morning I woke up and life for us changed but as a teen things did between us drastically. By then she was drinking alcohol. And my dad was a "wanna be", in and out of our lives. Not much else to say about him other than he was hardly around and a womanizer. I had begun to keep secrets. Who I hung with she didn't always approve of so I would sneak. The things I did after school and while out playing she couldn't know about because then she would punish me and I always wanted to be that same cute child she fell so in love with many years before. The one thing I could not hide was my anger. She would be called to many school meetings with the principle about me fighting. But it wasn't that apparent how malicious I could be until being expelled from Richmond Public schools system. It was then she began to pay heed that I had problems. So we endured months of psychological testing and anger management sessions. Yet while attending them I committed a crime that sent me away for my first stint of incarceration. When the police came to arrest me my Ma refused to let them take me because she swore it was not her son they were looking for. Her words exactly were "It couldn't have been my son because he was in the bed sleeping." She honestly had no idea I had snuck out of my bedroom window. But after some convincing and my giving up to them she let them take me in. We had a family attorney then and even though he was known by our entire family his fees were still expensive but my Ma spent her money time after time helping me. I was in a juvenile detention center for that crime. And my Ma would make the weekend trips there to see me. It didn't matter where I would go after that she would always be the one to do for me what I couldn't do for myself while incarcerated.

I write this because I need to see what I could not before as to the depth of a mothers love. Also that such a love as unconditional truly exist. I used to sell cocaine from my bedroom window. Even after she warned me that if I ever brought a gun into or sold and used drugs in her house I would have to find someplace else to stay. When she finally put me out it was not because she had stopped loving me as I thought then. It was because she didn't know me anymore and this scared her. The day my dad slammed me into a wall and I then went to my room and retrieved a weapon to kill him she had enough of tolerating my anger. To this day my dad doesn't know how close he came to facing my rage because she met me coming from my room and took the weapon away. Yet after some time had passed she let me back in. But by now I was embroiled in the usage of the very drugs I once sold and swore to never use. I was also drinking heavy and uncontrollably. My addiction and anger would take us on a downward spiral for many years after. I would steal from her to support my habit, one time taking her entire paycheck and spending it on drugs. The time I stole her stereo and t.v. while she stood calling me to come back and let her help me. Even though she grew tired of dealing with my antics she never gave up hope for her "son".

Today I know that she loves me beyond a shadow of a doubt because she always stood by me. Most of what I am revealing in Ghetto Blessings she never knew. Thinking about it now on the day when our cousin who was at that time a detective with the drug

and homicide unit came to her home and plead with me to get out
of the Southside Boys, she just looked with disbelief. But she still
loved me. This one thing is true. We talk now maybe not as much
as is necessary but enough to show we care. She tells me every
time how much she loves her "son" and how she prays for me. If I
am in a bind she doesn't hesitate to do what she can to help. No
matter the many times in and out of jails or rehabilitation centers
all I have to do is call and my Ma is there. Albeit Ma is not that
same beautifully young woman I first laid eyes on many years
ago but she is still so very beautiful nonetheless even moreso in my
heart. She still has hope that her "son" will be a man of
responsibility and production. She has never given up on me even
when I had given up on myself my Ma is there loving me and
blessing my life and heart with her patience, kindness, fortitude
and love.

Anger

I grew up around angry people. So much drunkenness and anger toward those they professed to love. My defining moment came the night my cousin and I sat on a roof top smoking "sherm" (PCP laced marijuana) and talking about life as I prepared my mental state for the challenge before me just mere minutes away as I would be "beat in" to the "A Disciples". I tried to focus on the anger I held toward people in my family that chose to abuse me and other members like it was acceptable. But my anger came from farther away. All I could concentrate on was what I would do to defend myself. My only thought was to grab a hold of someone and break their neck! Not to be easily beat in but with a fight. My cousin advised that I should not fight back he warned struggling back would only prolong the assault. But my mind had been made up long ago that I would fight tooth and nail to the bitter end. I was 10 years of age and had already begun exhibiting traits like my dad and step dad as for fighting. Only difference was they fought me and the women they loved while I fought other children. Fighting was a form of release and gave me a false sense of power being I had none to stop the beatings my mom and I took at home. Little did I know that the anger I harbored that night would grow more furious and intense as life moved on. I also believe if I had not struggled that night then maybe lot's of the issues I faced later on growing up an angry boy would not have transpired in the manner they did or I had become accustomed to.

My cousin looked me in the eyes and said, "Don't struggle."

But I did. I struggled because I was tired of being beaten. I struggled because I wanted to prove I was not afraid. The thing is I have been struggling every since. But today as a grown man I don't put my all into being uncanny angry. Of course I get mad. Even still have that urge to fight sometimes. But the actual process of getting angry and staying that way long after there is a need to be, has eased tremendously. I think it has to do with realizing with anger I am still trapped and allowing someone or something to control my emotions. So even though I struggle it's not the act of fighting to keep from being hurt, today I struggle to hold onto peace. Yeah. It is through peace I can sleep at night most times without nightmares of the past events that have scarred my conscience. With anger burning my soul and having no outlet I have nothing but misery because it has a way of strangling all the happiness my heart can feel at any given time. I prefer happiness over anger today. I prefer people being with me because they enjoy my company opposed to those being with me because they fear who I can be when angry.

A Prayer

"Dear Lord, I am thankful for life today. I am thankful for my health and strength that You so generously afford me each day. I thank you for watching over me and my family unfailingly. I thank you for giving me and blessing me, for Your love and tender mercy. My life and heart are filled with thanks because You have saved me from not only the things of this world that were destroying me but also from myself.

Lord, You know I am far from being righteous, still, You love me. You know my shortcomings and things about me that I choose not to divulge to anyone but are so apparent to You. And still..... You love and accept me. For this I am eternally grateful. You lift me up when I fall. Lord You give me fortitude when I am weak. It is by Your grace that I live and can hold my head up high and for all this, my soul sings Your praise.

I know in my mind I am not worthy to ask of You anything because I am a sinner and have done many horrible things. Yet You keep on blessing me while giving me those things I need daily. You give to me freely. You say that I can ask of You anything and I believe You will answer my prayers. I hurt so much inside sometimes Lord. But You are a healer of my wounds. I pray that You use me as a beacon. A light that shines through the foggy mist and guides someone out of the darkness. I pray that You use me and my experiences. Make me useful that my life is a testimony of Your goodness and salvation. That every word I speak be of You. So many people are in trouble Lord. So many people are losing life and freedom. I see everyday the children caught up in the whirlpool of destruction that is by no means a problem they should face alone, only they do. I see those living on the streets; those that suffer Lord and it breaks my heart that one time I was the cause of so much pain and loss. But now I ask You to touch them Lord as You have touched me. I ask You to heal our weary and forsaken land and its people. I know You can because

You did it for me. You saved me! Out of all those You could have, You did it for me because I asked. So now I pray that You do the same in the lives of those that ask of you and have faith in you.

Thank You for saving this wretched man and for giving me life again! Thank You for keeping me. Now Lord, teach me to live as You would desire me to; that I can be of service to you. That I may find richness in my spirit greater than any material wealth can ever be. Help me Lord to move on from my past and become a better man to myself and all those I encounter. Help me lord to love even those that love not themselves.

May You bless me, my family and friends. Bless the world.

In the name of Jesus Christ our Lord and Savior I pray these things.

Amen."

Molestation

He was a pillar in the community. A man well respected more from love than from fear of whom or what he was in the eyes of many. He was short and portly with a slightly balding head that always seemed to shine even in the dark. He was the pastor of the neighborhood church most that lived on the block attended including my family. He owned a corner grocery that also served as his home and would give credit groceries to many that lived on welfare and had no jobs. He was the only sponsor of our neighborhood youth football and basketball teams. His store was where I brought candy everyday before and after school. It was the one place in the community where kids hung out besides the playground and actually had fun. We would wait until closing then go to the rear of the store where he would meet us and hand out homemade cookies that weren't sold that day. Or the Kool - Aid ices he froze in little Dixie cups during the summer months just for us. I had become very fond of him as did many kids because he was like the dad we all wanted to have in our lives. Most of the kids had only a mother to be a parental figure in our lives. He would come to sport games, sit on the sideline and cheer us on. He would attend school functions and support our educational endeavors. I began to see him as someone that cared for me when my own dad was unable to. I guess it was fate that while in elementary school he would one day become my first employer and my worst enemy.

One day he came to our house and talked it over with my mom about me helping him at the store. He was old somewhere around 50 and the entire upstairs portion of the building was where he lived while the bottom floor was his store. He spoke of not being able to do all the cleaning and upkeep anymore and said he would pay me 25.00 a week to help run things in the store and do some occasional cleaning in his home. I believe if he had not been the man everyone saw him as my mom would have flat out said no.

But he was the preacher of our church for Christ' sakes! He had lived in this very community for years and everyone knew him as a sweet, caring man. No one saw the person he would become. I went to work and had been busy there for close to 3 months. The first time he asked me to hug him didn't register anything odd in my mind. I did and went home as usual. It didn't happen again until a couple weeks later but this time the tender embrace was more of a tight uncomfortable groping that scared me enough to tell my mom. She just said it was his way of showing how he appreciated my help and we left it at that. But when work was done and I would get ready to leave after that, I would not hug him. Instead I would find ways to leave before he had to let me out. Usually he would lock up then we would clean the display cases and as he would open the door after we were done. The first hug came as I was exiting; the second just before he opened the door. So I would plan ways to get by without him meeting me at the door. This worked for a few weeks until one day he just refused to open the door at all.

When I realized he had other intentions, a coldness formed in my heart that I have lived with ever since; that part that allows me to distance myself from feeling. A protective device that affords me to be cold hearted when faced with love or people that profess it. I find refuge in this because it has kept me safe from hurt. But it has also deprived me of completeness because I have accumulated many hurts in my life that were primarily caused by my own doing, simply because of fear. As I tried to leave he took me into his arms and carried me to the rear room of the store. It was there he had his way with me. The blessing was that just before he completely undressed me my mother knocked at the front door having stopped by to get me after work instead of me walking home alone that day. Even though he took time to get himself and me together before answering the door, my mom the way she looked at us both could tell something wasn't right. But neither of us said anything except "goodnight and see you tomorrow".

However after we arrived home I broke down in tears and had to tell her what happened. I expected her to call the police or go there and kick his ass or something. I could see by her expression she was angry but also there was a look of disbelief. I wanted her to find my dad. Wherever he was and tell him but she didn't leave the kitchen where we stood crying. It seemed like hours before she even came over and hugged me.

I was forbidden to go to that store again. I could no longer walk with my friends to school on the rout that took us pass it. And she would meet me when she could after school then we would walk the long way home together. We stopped attending his church as he stopped supporting and attending sporting events. I was sworn to silence, not even to tell my dad about what happened. Only my mom and I would have to carry the memory of that day. In the end only I have this weight to bear.

The word of God tells me "I will never put more on you than you can bear." It tells me, "Come unto me all who are weak and heavy burdened and I will give you rest." Many days after the incident, I had taken my life into my own hands. I had tried to be this super being that found ways to escape my burdens through drugs, violence and irresponsibility. I refused to look at the blessings of every single thing good or bad that transpired in my life because I felt nothing mattered. There were no "real" blessings in my hardened heart. Only wishes for things to come or take place in my life that would alleviate my misery. But truth is the biggest blessing of all came through my refusal to accept that out of everything in my life I held onto hope that one day my life would be better if I just kept faith it would. After all I have witnessed, only by the grace of God I no longer have to live like I once did. I don't have to harbor resentment for someone that hurt me because it is bearing my cross that I seek forgiveness and must give it as well in order to move on. I have been given reprieve from my own sins so what makes me think I can not forgive those whom have sinned against me. My life is more meaningful for understanding that we are all human and make mistakes. Some of us need professional help to overcome our shortcomings. Some commit crimes against innocent people and have no remorse but they are still human beings and their punishment will always be so much more than someone carrying vengeance can hold against them. In our life we are constantly being bogged down by so many things which deplete us of living and enjoying the life we have been blessed to have. Wow. I have a way to be free of that bondage today. Now I choose to struggle for freedom rather than struggle holding onto the ball and chain of my past. It is not easy. But anything in life worth having is also worth fighting for.

Where God Abides

I cry tears today.

I have awakened from nightmares of those no longer here calling my name.

I have seen death waiting like a vulture. Looming unawares, waiting patiently.

I wake up some nights sweating profusely.

I am afraid.

My life is often not the fairy tale depicted in my words of goodness and joy.

I question most times where did all the goodness go or if I am meant to have it at all.

I find it hard to forgive myself.

Yet I seek the forgiveness of others.

I get angry when faced with life and I have only one answer to a thousand questions.

I hide.

I hurt.

I smile.

I am fearless.

Still, I am afraid.

Every single day I am confronted by my past.

Everyday.

Just the same I know that God abides.

Because I live.

Prison

This was to be about the 3 years, 11 months and 22 days I spent incarcerated. For many years of my life I thought prison was that place surrounded by barbed wire fences and steel doors; those institutions that held people captive physically. But until I was incarcerated and still found I was bound did I realize prison of self is far worse. See, one can be released from an institution and still not be free. My spiritual prison is that which enslaves me to self pity, shame, degradation and pain. It is there were no such emotions as love exists. While serving time I was constantly around 500 men at any given time, yet I was alone. When I was diagnosed with a terminal illness, I used many peoples reaction to this disease as a means to build my prison walls higher. I held onto the heinous things I did in my past. The years of drug abuse, my dropping out of school, anything negative from my life I used as a means to remain imprisoned in my being. Not because I didn't want to be free, but because I didn't want to face what I had easily locked away along with my soul. Thus, I had to recognize prison for what it is if I ever truly mean to be free. There was a man I befriended while serving the last year of my sentence. He was early into the 15th year of a sentence which would keep him locked inside an institution for the rest of his natural life. But he would speak as if he wasn't even serving time. On the last day we talked he said this to me.

"I ain't ever getting out of here. I wouldn't even know what to do if I did. But you are going back into the world. Make the best of it son. Don't keep this place. Let it go. You have the chance to be free. Use it, because, even though I am in man's prison, God has set me free."

I strive through mercy and love to be unbound. I am not ashamed of the life I lived so I use this as a tool to open the eyes of those incarcerated within the prison of self that maybe they too will

come to see freedom. Perchance we all will come to understand
that life is a gift we only get one opportunity to open.

Cracked Lives

There was a time when I looked down on those living with drug addiction. A "crack head" to me was the vilest person imaginable that would do anything to get high. I never saw a "functioning" crack head, one that maintained responsibilities while entertaining usage. In the neighborhoods where I sold cocaine there was no separation. No one had a job that gave benefits like 401k or retirement options. Most didn't have jobs at all. Welfare was a main form of support. Selling to me and using drugs for crack heads lent a form of security. And the faster the money was made the more enticing the act; the more potent the drug the better the escape. People that had no job skill could sell drugs and without filling out an application or undergoing interviews that divulge their background. No college degree was needed, and you could dress anyway you chose. Work the hours you chose. No pre - employment drug test. Nothing associated with the normal daily grind of meaningful employment. All one had to exhibit was the nerve to sell illegal substances.

Even though I detested crack heads they were my sole means of wealth for many years. I however had a distant respect for the ones that hustled to support their addiction. The grimier the hustle, the more respect. I would give more cocaine to a "booster" (one that shoplifted) or someone hustling aluminum cans before I would women that sold their body for drugs. To me that wasn't hustling because every woman has that commodity that every man wants. It doesn't take much thought as to how she will get money besides what attire to wear while on the street. I think about how I would treat addicts just because they had no control over the chemical reaction going on in their mind; calling them names outside of what they were born with; degrading them for wearing the same dirty clothes or for living in abandoned buildings and smelling like urine. I would go ballistic when one would owe me the slightest amount of money, treating them like they weren't even human beings but animals that I controlled. Of course all crack heads weren't the same. They all had individual personalities. There were those that would do nothing but shoplift everyday; those that sold cans and drank alcohol; those that worked the labor employment services. Women that only sold their bodies as a last resort to get money rather pulled "tricks" (robbing customers) to get paid. The thing is I never saw myself becoming what they represented in my mind, "a useless individual controlled by a chemical".

Crack was always prevalent in the hood it just took on a different form at the onset. It was referred to as "free basing". Then the cocaine wasn't as diluted as it has become. But cracked lives were in full destruction no matter. Smoking cocaine has a way of dismantling rational thought. The euphoria associated with it takes people to distant plains of living. There was a crack head we called "Up" because before that crack hit he would be the saddest individual. But immediately after ingestion he would sing, dance and come alive like his life now had meaning and he was so happy. I would give him crack hits just to see him perform. Like I was his puppet master pulling his strings with crack hits. But this all changed the night I smoked free base for the first time. The thing is, I had tried many drugs before and most I never did again, like heroin and PCP. I did them once and didn't like the effect so never did them again. But the first time I smoked cocaine I immediately became hooked to it. Strangely, the first time I experienced the high I felt in my being that this was the worst thing I could ever do. I felt it would destroy me and was very afraid of what was happening to me mentally. Yet I didn't stop until many years later. In the rooms of Narcotics Anonymous there is a saying that one has to hit a bottom before they will finally take a look at stopping the destruction. Well I realize today that every time I put the crack pipe in my mouth, my bottom had been achieved. I didn't have to lose my home, car, job and family to see my bottom. All I have to do is use because what crack does to me is send me spiraling out of control like a wildly spinning top and I do not stop spinning until everything I own is gone, my heart, mind, body and soul.

I soon found company with the very ones I detested. They laughed at me in the beginning, but soon welcomed me as their equal. The dealers that knew me before would curse me and call me names. I was less than a person in their eyes just like so many were in mine before. I started shoplifting and stealing from those close to me. The gun I once carried for protection I now used for robbing innocent people and the weaker dealers. I became a pathetic liar. I wouldn't sleep until my body gave out and I would pass out from exhaustion. I found my way in and out of jails so much they knew me personally. My whole life was like some kind of awful nightmare that I couldn't wake up from. I now saw how crack heads truly lived on a daily basis. I lived in abandoned buildings, ate from trashcans, panhandled for money to get one more hit. No matter how disgusting the lifestyle, it was what we all did to survive and get high.

Today if I can tell one addict anything substantial it would be this

"We don't have to live cracked lives anymore. I know it's a hard habit to break but we have to want it broke more than the desire to keep self destructing through usage, though it may not seem like there is a way out....... though all may seem lost. We don't EVER have to use another substance again. We don't have to die in the streets. We don't have to be crack heads anymore. But first we must make the decision to change. Then have faith and determination that this change will happen. Once we open our life to change and adhere to it, everything we lost will be regained ten fold; most importantly our dignity and self respect."

A Lump of Coal

I was a lump of coal. One of thousands sitting in the heap waiting to be discovered.

Black and shapeless. Lumpy, covered by dirt and soot from the ashes of erosion and earth.

Devoid of purpose. Unattractive and even though surrounded by many pieces just like me. Still alone.

Then one day the hands of God.

The one greatest artist.

The creator of life.

His hands reached down into the mire and removed this beaten and unformed rock of coal.

He began to chisel away my hardened exterior that flaked and fell off with ease.

The more He chiseled the harder I got. The deeper He went into my being the more of a task it became to remove the crusty blackness of molten life.

Yet, He continued to work at this masterpiece, because in His eyes beneath all the dirt and grime something glorious lived.

His hands pressed and reconstructed.

Removing the grime and filth.

Then one day having gotten rid of the outer parts holding now a smaller tap, but still a piece of coal.

He used His finest tools from there.

Dawning a jewelers lens He meticulously carved and shaped.

Diligently He worked to rid my soul of all the hardness of the life I lived.

Then like a rock cutter He chipped off all the black exterior to reveal the most precious jewel.

His hands then designed and recreated the most brilliantly beautiful multi - faceted diamond.

Then like a parent ever so proud of the child that could do nothing wrong.

Like the parent finding pride in the child created from love.

He placed me upon a crown for all the world to see.

And smiled...... "This is My child, in whom I am now well pleased."

We are all lumps of coal. We all have our skeletons and shortcomings that hide or take away from the beauty we are meant to possess. Life has a way of hardening our hearts and minds. Many of us suffer. Many of us have no belief that there is any good in us. But like me, His hands are there waiting to form the most exquisite diamonds. All we have to do is let Him.

Ghetto Blessings: Redemption

Webster's defines "Redemption" as... 1. Redeeming or buying back. 2. Deliverance from sin. 3. Salvation.

1. I have to be willing to fight for the buying back of my life from those things that had purchased my soul as a slave. No more sitting and waiting for some great sign. No more talking about being tired of how my life is held captive. No more excuses. It is now time for war.

2. I had to seek deliverance from the sins I committed. To be freed from the wrongs of my past if I am to move toward my future. I had to ask forgiveness from those I hurt or manipulated. Then I had to find a way to forgive myself.

3. I had to desire to be saved from the life I lived which was tearing me apart and enslaving me. My desire is to be free.

I wrapped a teenage school mate in toilet paper and lit it afire, because he groped my then girlfriend and made her cry. The severity of burns covered 30% of his body and sent me away to a juvenile detention center for 1 year; costing my mom thousands in hospital bills and monthly expenses for me while incarcerated. I drove my car into a crowd of people then jumped out guns blazing coming to the aid of a fellow gang member during a fight. While all this took place children and innocent people scrambled about attempting to evade the wildly spraying gunfire. I have broken many hearts while taking the very meaning of love and turning it into a way for me to use people. That once I grew tired of playing the game I would dismiss them broken and hurting; like they were deserving of such behavior.

The point I'm trying to make is that I was a very bad person at one time in my life. I did some very nasty things to people. And as a result for many years of my life I felt there was no chance someone like me could ever be forgiven. I walked around cold and lifeless; missed out on many loves and happy endings because I held onto sadness, distrust and unfaithfulness. Thinking there was no other way. This is my journey. Ghetto Blessings is my look back at my life in order for me to see where it is through forward progress I must go. Only God knows the many days and nights I have cried and hurt so damned bad when confronted by my sins. The pain I still sometimes feel while looking at my face in the mirror is most times unbearable. Waking up from nightmares that leave me scared to sleep for days after. I am quick to say I have no regrets from my past but this is a lie to cover up my wrongs. The word of God says this," The wages of sin IS death." Before Ghetto Blessings I wrote for the vanity of my life. I thought of death as the physicality of no longer existing in this earthen vessel called a body. Today I realize the death I experienced was far more exceeding than mere physical expiration. I now have a different understanding for death and that which I was reborn from. See spiritual death was that which disabled me from having life. The death I underwent was imprisoning my being in a void where there was no escape. All the pain was a direct result of the emptiness I had in my life; all the destruction I caused many. I took the weight of everyone upon my shoulders and bogged down in shame finding my actions not only affected me but generations, communities, races and futures. Thus I was dead.

If you read this and find understanding of your own it will be apparent that my everyday is a struggle. I have a disease that claims thousands of lives daily. I am a convicted felon with a violent criminal past making it hard to find gainful employment. I owned a business that through my actions I lost. I have been through two divorces and the lost of my only child due to my neglect. Many people will never have the privilege of knowing their son and grand children because of me. I ride through neighborhoods ravished by drugs and shake my head from sadness because I was a part of drugs hitting those communities so hard.

Everyday I struggle. However, by the grace and mercy of the God I have come to understand and have faith in I know that everything I went through is His way of making me the man I am today. Everything I go through today is so I don't forget as I easily can sometimes where I came from. I write this today for two reasons; one that it is a form of healing to my soul; the other is that just maybe someone struggling also may find the truth that there is redemption from a life of sin. Let Ghetto Blessings rain upon the world and issue forth new fruit! Let it shower hope over the fields of arid poverty stricken slums where drugs, illiteracy, degradation, strife and social ignorance have taken blessed and wonderful people hostage. May we all find salvation of some kind from the lives we are accustomed to upholding through negativity and destruction. I pray this be the fuel that ignites a fire to fight for those things which give us spiritual richness instead of materialistic gain. May God bless us all.

Miracle Lessons: The Blessings Unfold

Miracles. Those acts of amazement that happen unexpectedly and give new perspectives on life; the unseen questions that arise. How and why certain things came to take place. The terminally ill person that one day awakens healed of their affliction; receiving help when none is present.

At one time in my life these random acts of goodness were looked at as lucky encounters or coincidences; those stories from the bible of acts performed by God. However, with each incident I am about to divulge I hope we all see the true form of miracles, that we may understand they are very real and God is still in the capable of performing them.

The first time I witnessed a miracle just like everyone else that was there it merely seemed to be a lucky chance. Nothing important about it except I survived because the car I flipped several times into oncoming traffic hitting 8 other vehicles was made of steel and sheltered me from harm. I walked away unscathed. Not even a scratch while in the same instance a 56 year old woman was nearly killed. My mom and grand mother mentioned "God having His hands on me". I smiled and chalked it up to luck. Miracle? The next time one occurred while standing in a parking lot talking to a then business associate and a rival gang member opened fire at me with a semi automatic firearm from a distance of about 5 feet. I looked directly into his eyes as the firearm leveled at my head. I heard the shot. Saw no possible rout of escape, nothing in this world could have protected me from death. Mysteriously the first shot missed. The assailant charged as I turned to run for cover behind my car. "POW! POW! POW!", the gun blazing and not a single bullet hit me. I looked from the ground beneath the car to see his feet coming toward me and my associate. I knew my life was through. Looking up and seeing the rival now standing over me, I could see shock in his eyes. More like confusion. He just had this awkward gaze before running off.

Once again my life was spared. All I received was a graze across my head. All that witnessed this cried and wailed thinking I had been shot several times. The associate looked at me, shaking his head furiously in disbelief; so shaken by what transpired he had to be sedated after the paramedics arrived. So many events from my life would raise the attention of theorist as to the actuality of miracles taking place; or just coincidences? One night I was "pistol whipped" and left for dead having suffered a concussion, broken ribs, nose, and bleeding profusely in an abandoned house after being robbed by a gang of ruffians. Somehow I was taken to a store where the owners called paramedics and they got me to a hospital. I awakened hours later to see my wife standing over me crying, trying to keep me calm after I'd been strapped to a gurney because the emergency room personnel said I would briefly gain consciousness and begin yelling that I would kill them and swinging wildly. Weeks later I returned to the abandoned house. Over every wall were splatters of my blood. On the carpeted floor where I lay dying there was a matted, dark crimson blot of dried blood that soaked through the carpet staining the hardwood flooring underneath. My eyes filled with tears and I thanked God for however method He rescued me. Then finally years later the night I was so distraught and beaten mentally, physically, spiritually and emotionally I put a loaded gun to my head and pulled the trigger. Yet, I am here today writing this.

I want everyone that reads this to honestly think about the possibilities of miracles. Look around you at the trees and the sky. Take a trip to the mountains and the sea. Seriously examine your body and configure how everything works; the how and why. Go to a local hospital and view the newborn infants. Visit the sick and hear their stories of life out of illness. Then ask yourself "Do miracles exist and how can I not believe?". This is not an attempt to force anyone's beliefs to fit my own. I do believe beyond a shadow of a doubt that there is a God and He has seen fit to save my life many times through acts of amazement. I believe there is no man that can create any single living organism upon this planet. Very simply I believe in miracles. However, we are all far from the same. Thus this is written that just maybe someone will see things as I do; someone that couldn't see the miracles transpiring in their own life nor had a definition as to the events where they were spared from an untimely death. Then we are to find what our purpose for having survived is. That is the blessings unfolding. Where we learn from our mistakes and try and help someone to make rightful decisions that won't take them along the paths we have travelled.

Someone once said to me that "we are only lucky at horse shoes and gambling". I tend to believe that now because life isn't about lucky chances. Many have died through their involvement with incidents others have faced and walked away from. Only now that we have seen what will it take to believe. And once we believe what will it take to open our hearts and minds to help others reach the same conclusion that yes, miracles do happen. And there is only one being capable of performing them. God.

About The Author

Some will say I don't have the right to label people, places and things as is written in this works as "ghetto". However this label applies more to me than anyone because I've experienced what ghetto has come to represent in the eyes of so many Americans today.

I was raised modestly as an only child by many family members from diverse social and economic backgrounds and went from the streets of New York City and its five boroughs, to the rural country environment of a small town in Lynchburg VA. I grew from an angry, confused teen into a materialistically wealthy young adult, till in my latter years I became a hopeless crack addict, a homeless vagabond and lastly an inmate serving a prison sentence for all the crimes I committed.

Now I try and understand why I am afflicted by a terminal disease? I try and piece my life back together even though I often feel I have no time left. I wonder why at the age of 45 I have to return to my roots in order to move ahead and grow as a man. These are the words of my life they may be harsh at times even senseless but I have come to realize that it was all to make me who I am today.....and no matter what I thought then I know now it was all part of my blessing.

Also by Carlos Robinson...

Now that you have enjoyed Ghetto Blessings, Check out Carlos Robinsons first book "Open Heart Surgery".

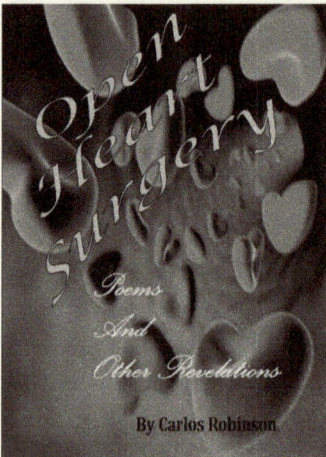

Excerpt From Open Heart Surgery

My Face....

I looked upon the aura of love and it called my name as if it has known me all my life. "Beautiful." that's what love called me with a voice so soft and demure. And like a surging wave against a fading shore I melted with tears.

"Why do you cry oh GREAT man of emotion? Have I offended thee in someway by stating your wondrous power to be as God created you to be?" Loves question struck discord within my soul because I never saw myself as beautiful and would not allow anyone else to see it either because then they would see it as weakness.

"Or do you cry from the pain of living your life and not until now knowing just who you really are as a man?" love continued.

In anger I shouted out from the very top of tainted lungs," I NEVER CRIED FOR LOVE BUT SURELY FROM THE PAIN! I NEVER CRIED FROM JOY, BUT SURELY FROM DISDAIN! WHAT IS IT YOU WANT FROM ME!?!"

And without a seconds hesitation loves answer is this...." I have never wanted anything of you that you're not capable to give,".....so strong her voice yet serene.

I began to sob woefully. Lamenting the distress of many years spent in loneliness. I bowed my head in shame and love tenderly lifted it then very gently like falling flakes of snow kissed my lips with a passion that calmed me for the moment; my heart pounding hard like drummers of some ancient ritual signifying the approaching battle to all surrounding tribes. I now smiled so brightly with confidence and pride! My longing for love had been given reprieve..... My emotions had finally been set..... Free, if only for that moment in time.

   Years have passed since that encounter and when I thought that day was merely a dream I realize now it wasn't. Love still kisses me and calls my name "Beautiful". It comforts me even though loneliness has built a prison around my heart.

   Love is always there. Waiting for me to accept it's real and to invite her into my life. Without being afraid or feeling unworthy to receive such a blessing. Love is everywhere and in everything but it can not be seen purely with carnal eyes. No..... this kind of love can only be seen with the eyes of one's heart."

www.ingramcontent.com/pod-product-compliance
Lightning Source LLC
Chambersburg PA
CBHW032022090426
42741CB00006B/697